A Year of Mystic Angels

by Dana

a.k.a.: Denise Iwaniw

The Temple Within llc
219 Glenview Court NE
Rockford MI 49341
www.templewithin.com

First Edition 2010©

ISBN: 978-0-9722002-8-8

Graphics: Wendy Mersman, Moon Designs, LLC
              www.MoonDesigns.com

          David Fix, Hearth Productions, LLC
              www.HearthProductions.com

Printed in the USA
Sentinel Printing Co.
St. Cloud MN 56304

To purchase The Mystic Angels Empowerment Deck
    Please visit: www.TheMysticAngels.com

Table of Contents

"The one known as Jophiel, am I.
The one known as a Child of Light, are you.
Feel the Light circuits in your bodies connect with the Light Circuits of the One*
Rest here.
Hold the Light.
Say to yourself…I am Love, I am Joy, I am abundance, I am song, I am eternal, I am wisdom,
I am laughter, I am dance, I am poetry, I am Nature, I am my brother, I am my sister,
I am Light, I am all that ever was, All that is, All that ever will be.
And so you are."

-St. Jophiel, Archangel

Dedication
Acknowledgments
Preface

Dedication

"As the sun sets on the horizon of your earthly home each evening,
may it serve as a reminder that each sun*set heralds a beautiful sun*rise at dawn.

Allow the sun to set upon those things in your life,
which are no longer of use to your Journey.
Bless their purpose and vision them setting like the sun…fading from view,
disappearing with love.

In their stead, vision the sun rising, gloriously anew!

Dancing upon each ray of the emerging sun,
see all of your hopes, your dreams, your joys,
and imminent miracles becoming Reality.

Breathe them in.

Exhale them into Life ~*

You, like the rising sun, are the living vision
of Hope, Dreams, Joy, Love, and Miracles of the Creator!

In this knowing, dance upon the rays of Life!
Hope, Dream, Laugh, and create Miracles…they are a reflection of You.

Rest well. Play well. Love well.

Here comes the Sun…"

-St. Uriel, Archangel
May 4, 2009

"Without even looking at the pages I want you to know yes, I would love to edit your chapters."
That was the written response I received from my Dominican Earth Angel, Sister Irene Mary,
when I asked her if she might once again, edit my work.

I am eternally grateful for her and her belief in me.

On many levels, Irene Mary, whose very name means, 'Peaceful Star of the Sea', is the
personification of the joy, faith, and strength that I call upon each day that my earthly body walks
this astral plane called Gaia.

This book is dedicated entirely to her.

Acknowledgments

"Upon and within the fullness of your Being lies Celestial Light supreme.
Look not outwardly, but within your innermost dwelling for the One who loves you most of all.
Once discovered, you shall learn to love yourself, as the Creator loves you; with unconditional
love, endless compassion, and with a Joy that knows no bounds."

-St. Uriel, Archangel

This book is written for my fellow beings of Living Lightness, who are at this moment, in the process of Awakening to their true Nature.

Following the publication of, Embracing the Mystic Within, I was asked almost immediately, when my next book would be released. I had no clear answer. None was given when I asked Spirit. That was, until today.

As a writer, I think it's rather natural to wonder what sort of writing might lie ahead. Each time I wondered, I was left wondering why there appeared to be nothing to answer that question. Just a whole lot of wondering and a whole lotta nothing.

At 10:11 a.m. on May 4, 2009, all of that changed.

A choir of joyful Angels directed me to sit in my chair and begin typing.

"Just listen." They chimed.

Listen, I did.

What unfolds within these pages is a culmination of spiritual teachings, personal readings, divine messages, and psychic calisthenics to help your universal heart expand, your wings unfurl, and your Lightness to shine!

It is after all, all about the Light of the Great Central Sun within and our connection to the Great Central Sun without.

Together, we are called to shine.

My sincere gratitude goes out to the clients, family, and friends who have allowed me to share their stories within these pages. Out of respect for their privacy, I have changed their names throughout this book.

Many thanks to Eunice Norwood, who readily agreed to proofread this entire project. Thank you, Eunice, for shining your splendid Light upon this work. It shines for all to see.

In the Spirit of Light, Divine Happiness, and Infinite Gratitude to the Blessed Mother and Her multitude of Light Angels, I offer this volume.

In Joyfull Awareness that We Are Living Light*,

Dana

Preface

"Blessed are they who endeavor to find the Light*,
though they walk through the shadow of the illusion known as darkness.
They understand their True nature.
Blessings be to those who show the way, and hold the hearts of those lost in darks' illusion.
They are the Lightshowers*
Blessings rain upon those who hold the Light* despite the illusion of chaos.
They understand that ALL things emanate from the great Lightness*"

-Sandalphon, The Archangel

Angels come and go. Sometimes they stay. In either case, Angels are always all around. I choose to capitalize the word Angel, because to me, they are beings of the Highest Order, deserving of their capital A. After all, even an Angel can appreciate a little respect from a mere mortal, like me.

They laugh in my ear as I type those last few words.

"Mere mortal?" they chime in.

"Yep," says me.

"Honestly, Dana, you've not forgotten from whence you came, have you? While we choose to remain in the ethereal planes of inner dimensional being, mere mortals like you have chosen to subject yourselves to the earthly grading school of ascended learning. Nothing mere about that, after all."

I ask myself, "Do Angels, really say things like...from whence you came?"

The celestial voices continue...

"The day to day and night to night routine of capturing you when you stumble or fall can indeed become tiring for us. Lending a shoulder to cry on, or swooping in to lend first aid to a broken heart, can be weary work. Of course, there are those times when we try diligently to get your attention, through signs and wonders, only to be ignored. Very frustrating, indeed. It's not easy being an Angel. Despite our glorious wings of Light and serene appearance, the job requires stamina and determination.

Most of all, it requires a great deal of unconditional love, which we have in abundance. It's the stuff we're made of. Good thing. A great deal of Love is required to nurture what you term a mere mortal.

We are joyful that it is you and not us that have taken on the task of mortal living. Living Lights in mortal flesh are very brave.

Mere mortals are Living Lights. Courageous, Living Lights."

And onward still…

"For the next 365 days, we will guide you in this writing endeavor and converse with you about Heavenly, as well as merely mortal matters. It is our wish to remind you of your Lightness of Being and of the valor that is your natural makeup, during the earth walk.

We shall appear to you in many colorful guises. Our discourses will be delivered via seen and unseen High*ways. The messages will be given to you, through you, for you, and all who read these many pages.

Our task is to help you remember the times when we have appeared in your life. Through stories and wise-doms, we will make our point of showing you how very real we are and how very much we love you, and others, through you. Since most Living Lights* have forgotten that they are beings of such divine stature, we have no choice than to work through those Lights* who have always known, or recently remembered.

For those who have recently Awakened and those who can't for the life of them remember their Lightness alike, we shall provide soul exercises in remembering. Most of them will be fun, some challenging, all of them Loving calisthenics of the ascended kind."

"Ready, Dana?" they sing.

"Ready as I'll ever be." I think.

"You've always been ready," they remind me.

"Oh yea, that's right." I know.

"Okay then…let us begin," we say in synchronistic Lightness of being…

"Miracles are seen in light.
The body's eyes do not perceive the light.
But I am not a body. What am I?"

A Course in Miracles, Lesson 91

Chapter One
Children of the Light*

hat am I?" A common question, with an uncommon answer.

Most people, I believe, answer that question with a dry statement that delineates their worldly profession. Such a response might include: "I am a nurse, I am a graphic designer, I am a waiter, I am a pilot, and I am a teacher."

Others may have a more tentative, if not fearful, response that might sound a little something like this: "I am an aspiring artist, I am a hopeful singer, I am a want to-be author, I am a diamond in the rough, waiting to be polished and shined."

Of course, we all know that cocktails and dinner conversation always lead to the standard question, "So, what do you *do*?"

If the Angels had their way, anyone who is ever asked the question, would heartily and enthusiastically respond in this manner; "I am a Child of the Light, conceived and born of the Light, in order to carry the Light, and to shine It brightly."

When was the last time you heard *that* response at a dinner party?

Now then, if you were to ask a young child, who might have invited you to attend their tea party, the very same question, while mixing and mingling with well groomed baby dolls, festively dressed teddy bears, and *imaginary friends,* the answer might very well reflect another tone of reality.

Children remember.

Before grown ups and the material world can fill their crystalline minds with adult nonsense, the little ones remember where our true home is. They know where they came from and where they will return one day.

In their innocence, they remember that *home*, like the Emerald City in the Land of Oz, is always near, and that we never really leave home at all, except to visit far off places, like the playground on earth.

Five year old Brittany was introduced to me by her mother, Sandra. With a delicate face like a fairy princess, and long, flowing black hair to frame it, she sat across from me in the large white wicker chair. Her mother, confused about her daughter's visits from spirit, sat next to her in a matching chair, nervously biting her nails.

Sandra began our session by telling me, "Since the time Brittany was about two and a half years old, she started to describe seeing spirits. Without ever meeting my mother in real life, she was able to describe her 'Nana' in great detail. When I asked her how she knew Nana looked that certain way, she told me very frankly that it was because Nana visits her during the day and sometimes at night. She was so serious and exact in her description, that it made me take notice.

To find out if she was really seeing my mom, I took an old photo album out of the closet and removed a family picture from one of the sleeves. This particular photo has several members of my family pictured in it. When I showed the old snapshot to Brittany, I asked her if she could tell me which person in the group photo was Nana. Without hesitation, she pointed directly to my mother. I was stunned."

"How did that make you feel, Sandra?" I wanted to know if it frightened her.

Sandra's eyes welled up with tears, "At first I was scared. Then I cried, because I knew that in some way, my mother had been able to let Brittany know that she was still alive on some level in some place that I can no longer see. Believe it or not, I used to be able to see things when I was a child, too. It scared me though, so I asked *it* to go away and it did. Now I wish I could see those things again."

Turning to the little raven haired psychic sitting across from me I asked, "Brittany, can you tell me what other things or people you see, if any?"

Shyly hugging her lavender teddy bear and looking over at her mom, she worked up the courage to explain that not only can she see her Nana, but she also sees beautiful Angels and boys and girls who sometimes come into her home.

Her bright brown eyes widened as she responded, "Their mouths move, but I can't always hear what they are saying. Sometimes they walk toward me with their arms reaching for me, and it scares me."

One small girl in particular, stood out in Brittany's memory.

"Mommy and I were sitting on the couch watching TV one night when a little girl with blonde hair and a flowery dress came into the room with us. The little girl was walking toward me with her arms out like she was trying to get me. I told her to stop scaring me. When I did that, she stopped and asked me, "Brittany, am I dead?" I told her that she must be dead because my mommy couldn't see her. Only I could see her."

"What did you do then?" I asked.

Looking down at my carpeted floor, she responded, "I asked for my Angel to come and help her."

"Did your Angel come to help?"

In a now quiet voice Brittany looked up at me and said, "Yes. It was very beautiful. The little blonde girl was smiling and my Angel held her hand. Then they were gone."

She continued, "Angels have wings and they smile all the time. I like Angels."

While her eyes were looking directly into mine, I smiled and said, "Brittany, you have been given a wonderful Gift from God, and you did the right thing, sweetheart."

Hearing my approval, her precious Angelic face lit up.

Sandra and her daughter went on to tell me about the spirit visitors that come to see her while she is in school and at church. They even come to play outdoors with her.

Listening to Brittany talk about the kids on the playground that no one else could see, reminded me very much of my own childhood. The visits from silent and unseen playmates were part of my every day reality, too. Like Brittany, I kept this information mostly to myself. I only told mom and dad once.

The five year old girl within me had found a friend with common experiences in the five year old child sitting across from me. Inside of myself, I was smiling.

"Do you talk to them?" I inquired.

"Yes, she responded, sometimes in my head and sometimes, when I'm alone, I talk out loud. Sometimes they try to talk back. Mostly, they just look at me."

Wanting to know how best to help, I asked them both, "Why did you come to see me today? How can I help you?"

Not surprisingly, trying to understand her daughter's other worldly experiences was number one on Sandra's list of reasons for our time together.

I explained to Sandra and Brittany, that they are 'psychic sensitive'. In other words, they are capable of perceiving the energy of people around them on the physical plane of existence as well as the non-physical plane of existence.

"You have been given an extraordinary Gift of Spirit." I declared with a smile.

They smiled brightly in return.

Although Sandra had banished her Gifts to an unknown realm as a young child, her daughter was now experiencing them, just as she had. In fact, Brittany's experiences were much more profound and frequent.

Many believe, as do I, that spiritual Gifts are part of a familial lineage. Psychic parents give birth to psychic children.

Telling someone that you or your child can hear voices however, might still raise an eyebrow or two. Thankfully, as we progress as a race of spiritual beings having a human experience, all of that is changing.

From the many television shows and movies that deal with psychic happenings, spirit communication and ghost hunting in a practical manner, to best selling authors and public figures that are willing to address the subject, arcane notions about the Gifts of Spirit are fading away.

What was sometimes diagnosed as schizophrenia by uninformed medical providers decades ago, has now been given another look. Modern day physicians and psychologists are becoming highly educated in the areas of spiritual or psychic phenomena; in many cases, as a result of their own supernatural experiences!

Schizophrenia is a legitimate mental illness.

Spiritual phenomenon, on the other hand, is a direct result of our Origin.

We are Spiritual Beings having a *human* experience; souls within physical bodies.

An enlightened psychiatrist in this Aquarian age clearly knows the difference between Divine communication and a mind that is in a state of imbalance.

Currently, there is an influx of children who are arriving on this earth plane with spiritual gifts that are fully in bloom, to parents who have either forgotten their own gifts, or like Sandra, told them to go away, as a frightened young child.

From the three year old toddler who can clearly recall past lives, to the six year old who can remember the 'baby waiting room' prior to birth, we are seeing beautiful young Light Showers* bringing Heaven to earth.

Take four year old Seth, for example.

Speaking before a large crowd of psychic kids, their parents and grandparents, I asked the audience a question, "Has anyone in this room ever seen an Angel before?"

No sooner had the words departed from my lips, than Seth raised his cherubic hand high up in the air.

"Seth, I asked, would you like to share a story with us?"

"Yes!" he stated, through a broad, chubby smile.

Then, in a sweet, enthusiastic, four year old voice, this curly haired toddler began his Angelic encounter story. "Before I was born, I had an Angel. The Angel stayed with me all the time. I kept asking the Angel when I was going to get to see my mommy. He kept telling me, "Pretty soon, Seth." Every day I asked my Angel. Then, my Angel said, "Okay Seth, you get to see your mommy today!" Then, I was born and I got to see my mommy! And when I got to my mommy, the Angel was right there, too! He told me that he had to make sure I was okay. I was so happy to see my mommy. Now, here I am!"

Certain that everyone else in the room would want to know, I asked, "Do you still see that Angel, Seth?"

Leaning forward from his first row seat, firmly perched with hands upon his dimpled knees, he smiled once again and loudly declared, "Yep!"

The sounds of happiness and clapping filled the air.

A look of joyful knowing covered Seth's winsome face. His Angel, I could see, was indeed standing nearby him; lovingly protecting its young charge. It was an Angelic scene repeated throughout the room. Each person was sitting in the company of their celestial Guardian.

Seth's mom, like the other parents and grandparents in the room, brought their young relatives to my workshop not only to find out about the inner workings of their little intuitive, but to also have them meet other children who are sensitive, just like them.

Six year old Alexis, sporting two long, dark brown hair braids, with beautiful eyes to match, came to class with her mother. Her dad was still at work.

Mom was feeling troubled because Alexis can see not only Angels and departed loved ones, but also has the ability to hear animals and tree spirits speak. I referred to her as a young, female St. Francis of Assisi, in the making.

While diligently coloring a picture of a mighty oak tree, during our activity time, she looked up at me and said, "Denise, I have a famous saying that I made up. I say it to myself every day. Would you like to hear it?"

Knowing that her famous saying was certain to be a treat, I excitedly replied, "*Yes*, Alexis, I would love to hear it."

"Well," she began, "Here's how it goes…If you love everything that has a Spirit, *everything* that has a Spirit will love you back. *And*, since God gave everything a Spirit, *every* living thing will love you back."

With a smiling heart, I replied, "Bravo, Alexis! Beautifully said."

"You know, she continued, trees can talk. They talk to me every day."

"They do?" I asked.

"Oh yes. The maple tree at the corner of my driveway at home for example, waves at me when I am walking toward it after school. It's happy to see me! I give it a hug every single day. The tree knows that I love it."

After a moment of contemplative silence, still decorating her mighty oak tree with colored pencils, Alexis went on to ask, "Denise, did you know that different kinds of trees have different voices? And…they have different kinds of animals that like to live on them?"

I asked her to elaborate on that thought.

Her lesson to me began… "Well, robins like to live in maple trees and so do squirrels. They are happy there. Crows like to live in big old oak trees. Sometimes, animals live inside old oak trees that are hollow in the middle, too. Like raccoons and bunny rabbits. Little birds, like finches, like to live in pine trees. They feel safe there."

"Why do they feel happy and safe in certain trees?" I asked of my youthful St. Francis.

"Because the trees tell them that they are welcome to live there, and they will protect them," she answered.

I'm not certain how I could have missed such an obvious answer, but I delighted in the assuredness with which Alexis responded to my question.

During our entire conversation, her mother sat directly across from me, right next to Alexis. She listened in silence as her daughter and I discussed the magnificent spirits contained within trees, flowers, rocks, and stars.

"Has Alexis always had the ability to listen to the voices of the animals and Mother Nature?" I wondered out loud.

Her mother smiled and gently replied, "Yes. As long as I can remember, she has been hugging trees and telling me what she believes our pets are thinking. Animals have always been drawn to her. She's never had a fear of them, either. It's almost as though they know she can communicate with them."

Michelle went on to say, "I know that Alexis is unique and special. She has a Gift. The problem is that I don't want anyone or anything to get in the way of who she is. You know, to block her from using her abilities."

She then uttered the sentiment that many of the other parents and grandparents had shared with me that evening, "Denise, I am so happy to see lots of other children who are having these same experiences and delighted that they can all get together like this. It's so important for them to know that they are not alone. It's important for their parents, too."

In all of the aforementioned cases, these spiritually gifted children are exercising their psychic or soul awareness. As Alexis so beautifully worded it, they are of the knowledge that God has given everything a spirit. More importantly however, they understand that this God given spirit is alive, capable of receiving and giving love.

Throughout the evening, I watched the children.

For those who were unable to share their mystical experiences, due either to physical disabilities or the inability to form concrete statements about them, I provided opportunities for them to draw or color what they see and hear.

In addition to the use of their spiritual sensitivity, each silent artist created their divinely inspired stories through the use of colored crayons, pencils, markers, and paper. Ultimately, their creations left me, and their adult companions, in a state of joyful awareness. These youthful Living Lights* were experiencing the vastness of the Creator's loving presence around and through them.

No longer, did anyone feel alone.

Unconditional Love in its physical and non-physical forms filled The Center that night. Hearts that arrived anxious or empty, left full and content. Heaven had expressed itself fully, on earth.

So, what then, do we tell spiritually gifted children who are having experiences that are frightening? How can we calm their fears? Can we teach them to make troublesome and unwanted visitors go away?

In the autumn of 2007, a pleasant young man named Scott presented himself to me, along with his mother, for a private meeting. Much to the horror of them both, 13 year-old Scott was actually feeling what seemed to him to be fingernails scratching him along his arms and his legs. Although no physical markings were appearing on his skin, the definite sensation of 'scratching' was occurring.

Needless to say, he was altogether frightened. To make matters worse, neither mom nor dad could help him to understand what was going on.

It was during a conversation in which she revealed the nightmarish details of her son's experiences to her close friend, Kathy that Andrea was told about my book, *Embracing the Mystic Within*. Following the death of her own mother, Kathy found comfort in the book, and thought perhaps it might also shed some light on the experiences of Andrea's son, Scott.

Andrea agreed, and began to read the book. In the midst of reading it, she started to feel hopeful that I might be able to help them further understand Scott's bizarre experiences. After calling my assistant, a meeting time was agreed upon, eventually bringing me to the question that I would first ask him.

"Can you see whoever it is that is doing this to you, Scott?"

"No, but I can feel them. Kinda like a heavy presence. I can kinda almost feel them breathing by me," he offered.

"*Whoever* it is, they want me to know that they are there. I know that's why they touch me," he continued.

Investigating further, I asked, "Do you tell them to stop it?"

"No, I just kinda freak out and wave my hands in the air to bat them away. I don't know what to do. Who is doing this to me, Denise, and why are they doing it? My father thinks I'm making this all up to get attention. My mother believes me because she's my mom and because she had things happen to her when she was a kid too!" he exclaimed.

Looking at mom I inquired, "Andrea, what sorts of things did you experience as a kid?"

Sheepishly at first, she responded, "Well, you know the little things that go bump in the middle of the night; crazy dreams here and there; knowing when things were going to happen before they did. Stuff like that. They scared me to death. It scared my parents, too."

"Have these experiences continued into your adulthood?"

Emphatically she replied, "Heck no. I told God that whatever was going on, I wanted it to stop and it did! I was happy back then that it ended. Right now, I wish it hadn't stopped so that I could understand it better and help Scott. I feel helpless."

I'd heard those words spoken by many desperately searching parents before her.

Realizing just how upset Andrea was, I called for a momentary break, while I fixed a fresh kettle of hot water for chamomile tea.

Ten minutes and two cups of hot herbal tea in my hands later, the three of us re-convened. As Scott drank a bottle of cool, refreshing water, we began to sip on our soothing tea, and I continued our conversation.

"I just want you both to know," I began, "that neither one of you is crazy, possessed by wild demons, or imagining things that just aren't real. Your experiences are very, very real. The fact that both of you are sensitive to spirit, is simply an expression of your spiritual gifts."

It was apparent that no one had ever described events such as they were experiencing as a manifestation of spiritual gifts.

"The trick to managing your spiritual life is no different than the way we should structure our physical life. By setting boundaries in both realms, we help to create a safe distance with those who might choose to harm us, or at the very least, bother us. Do you understand what I'm trying to say?" I asked.

Both nodded in the affirmative.

I explained to Scott and Andrea that all things in the Universe are made up of energy. More than that, they are made of the energies of opposite polarities. Call them good/bad, high/low, loving/hateful, dark/light, Angelic/demonic, intelligent/ignorant, ultimately they all come from the same God source, which is Love.

If God created all things under Heaven and on earth, then all things come from God; even the scary stuff.

To answer Scott's question regarding the 'thing' that was touching him and why, I went on to say:

"Darkness is simply an absence of Light. Like moths to a lamppost, low vibration people, both physical and discarnate, are typically drawn to the Light. On the physical realm, they can be likened to the energy draining relative or friend who calls on you to make them feel better over and again. On the non-physical realm, it can be the case of a low vibration ghost who wishes to touch your Light body in order to experience Love. In both cases, it's your high vibration Light/Love energy that they wish to touch."

After assuring Scott that the entity on the other side only wanted to get his attention and to feel his Light, he seemed relieved.

"Just as you should express your dismay to the bully on the playground," I continued, "you should also express your upset to the spirit who is making your life uncomfortable. Stand up for yourself and tell them to go away. Let them know that they have no power over you. If you feel as though you need a little more muscle power behind your statement, invite an Angel of Light to be present with you, when you confront your bully."

"Because of your Gifts, the energy body that surrounds your physical body radiates a Light that can be seen throughout the cosmos. This aura Light body tells all unseen living things that you have the ability to perceive them. You can think of it as being something like a Lighthouse on two feet. Your sweeping Light penetrates the darkness, offering safe harbor to all those in need of Light and understanding. Sometimes, even a ghost needs a little understanding; a shoulder to lean on. When it becomes uncomfortable or frightening however, it's time to stand your ground," I concluded.

By understanding what our children are experiencing spiritually, adults are better equipped to handle the mental, emotional, spiritual, and sometimes physical interaction between kids and their spirit encounters.

Watching an infant gaze about a room, grinning from ear to ear at the seemingly empty air, or a toddler point and giggle in the direction of nothingness, can be confusing to someone unfamiliar with mystical matters.

If you, the reader, have a child in your life that is experiencing spiritual phenomena, take time to talk to this child about their experiences. Let them express to you, in their own way, what is going on.

Children, exercising their Gifts of Spirit, will describe in great detail, the sights, sounds, smells, and feelings associated with their experiences. They can describe even their invisible playmates with great fervor and accuracy. If you've ever watched a young child interact with their unseen friends, you've witnessed first hand just how real the encounter is.

Who exactly, are they playing with, you might ask?

Visitations by spirits that have a malevolent manner, as in the case of Scott, are rare. Anything that is *less than loving* is communication that is **not** of the Highest Order. I will address that subject in upcoming chapters.

Typically, young children are interacting with their Guardian Angel(s) or a loved one who has crossed over.

Our Guardian Angel(s) has been with us since the birth of our Soul. Because young children have not been living on the earth plane long enough to forget or block out their celestial companion, they see and hear them much more readily than their adult counterparts.

In the case of our departed loved ones, it is the loving ties that bind that keep them near their relatives. Similar to Angel encounters, children, in their untainted innocence, remain open to the loving vibrations of their family members who have returned to their pure spirit energy form.

I teach children that our physical bodies are *naturally* designed to receive spiritual information, as well as give it. We were created by a loving God, who wishes to remain active and interactive in our lives.

The way in which we 'perceive' the interaction of Spirit in our lives is unique and individual. Everyone experiences the Divine in his or her own way. In my previous book, *Embracing the Mystic Within*, I write at length about and refer to these unique spiritual abilities as, "The Clairs:"

- ❖ Clairvoyance – Clear Vision
- ❖ Clairsentience – Clear Feeling
- ❖ Clairaudience – Clear Hearing
- ❖ Clairosmesiance – Clear Smelling
- ❖ Clairgustiance – Clear Tasting
- ❖ Claircognisance - Precognition

For example, when we pray in silence, we are using our 'body antenna' to send a message to God. When we feel, see, or hear God answer us in prayer, we are using our 'body antenna' and our 'clairs' to *receive* the Creator's response.

Along those same lines, Angels were given to us by our loving Creator, not only to guide and guard us, but also that we might receive Divine messages through them; hence their name, which derives from the word, Angelos, or messenger.

It's important to let children of all ages know that God speaks to us in Loving ways. My favorite celestial equation is this:

GOD = LOVE

What follows on the coming pages are stories, Angelic love letters, sacred mantras and spiritual exercises designed to help you encounter and explore the Divine, in your own unique, Child-of-the-Light-like way.

With that in mind, it's time to take out your colored pencils, markers, crayons, and paper. Let's play, create, and explore the depths of our childlike wonder with Spirit.

Chapter Two
The Planes of Existence

The Astral Plane

In order to visit us, where exactly do the Angels and the spirits of our loved ones come from? Where are they, in relationship to us?

Both are questions that I'm quite often asked.

Let's begin with where *we* are; on what is called the astral plane.

"I've just closed my eyes again, climbed aboard the dream weaver train…"

At the age of 14, I was fond of listening to Gary Wright sing the lyrics to his song, "Dream Weaver." The year was 1976, and his song was a #1 hit on the U.S. pop music chart.

Aside from the deep, celestial sounding music, the words to this song struck a chord within me. A young teenager, I knew I was psychic. I also knew that beyond the highway of fantasy, there truly was a reality that people like me could tap into.

Following three decades of self education on the subject, and a stream of magnificent teachers that Spirit has so graciously provided for me, I have determined that while ultimately all reality stems from and is unified with the One Reality, our spirit traverses many levels or layers of the unseen world.

In the coming pages, I have attempted to delineate from my own experiences and personal research, the various planes of vibratory reality that all of Creators' living expressions exist upon and within. This delineation is merely created to give our brain a reference point about something that our soul already knows.

If we begin to think of our souls as having descended from the pinnacle point of Luminous Light called God, having gently pushed ourselves into lower, denser vibrations until ultimately we find our Light body clothed in flesh and bones on the third dimensional realm, we understand that throughout these various layers, live other members of Creation, who like us, are an emanation of the original One.

Finding ourselves however, in the third dimensional reality of earth's playground, we find that not all of our playmates are of the high vibration sort, like those we find in the highest of vibrations back Home.

Beginning with the densest forms of energy on the Physical Plane, we find solid objects, such as the black ergonomic chair I am currently sitting on and the beautiful mahogany desk that my computer keyboard is resting on. All of these items look and feel as though they are solid matter. In reality, they are made of matter being held together by the vibratory rate of their molecular makeup.

Some folks might even throw rocks and crystals into this very same category, labeling them as inanimate objects with no clear sign of life and therefore, having no intrinsic value.

Contrary to that belief, stones and crystals are very much alive with the Light and wisdom of Source. Grandfather stone, or Inyan, as he is called in Lakota, is not only alive, but like his brothers and sisters, the crystals, he is capable of healing people and animals with his unique life force energy.

As a record keeper, Inyan has been known to tell stories on behalf of our Earth Mother, Unci Maka. If you have ever taken the time to sit upon a large stone and listen to it recount the history of Creation, or tell you the tale of its existence, you know what I am talking about. For those who are in need of 'grounding' energy, sitting upon a stone and consciously absorbing its earthly vibrations will quickly bring you back into a balanced state between heaven and earth.

In the inipi purification ceremony, widely known as a 'sweat', Grandfather stone is heated up in a sacred fire until his prehistoric face shines brilliant red and his surface sparkles with life. Once he is placed in the shallow pit located at center of the inipi, water is poured from a ladle and herbs are gently placed upon his surface, creating a hot, cleansing steam. In this way, Grandfather Inyan gives his life to provide the intense heat and steam that rises up and through the inipi door, carrying the prayers of the faithful to Tunkashila, the Great Spirit.

Trees are some of my very favorite people. I like to call them librarians or legend keepers. Each one is a unique and individual being, serving as a living witness to the history of life all around it, all the while creating a safe harbor for wildlife to dwell upon and within it.

One of the best ways to have a conversation with a tree is to sit on the ground with your spine resting against its trunk. As your spinal chakras begin to align with the life force of the tree, you may feel, see, smell, or hear the Spirit of the tree speaking to you. If you listen with your heart, you will hear an account of life from the perspective of a wise old earth sentinel.

In the Disney animated movie, *Pocahontas*, the scene in which the ancient face of Grandmother Tree takes form upon her bark-like skin and speaks her wisdom to Pocahontas, is delightful in its representation of this. Grandmother reminds us that every rock and every creature is alive, has a name.

Listening to the timeless voice of Brother Wind rustling between the branches and blowing through the leaves on a tree, reminds us that all life around us, speaks to those who are willing to hear.

Living upon and within the forests, mountains, oceans, rivers, and streams, even in your own back yard garden, the Spirits of Nature take on many shapes and forms.

From mermaids to gnomes, undines to faeries, pixies to sylphs and salamanders, these are but a few of the many spirits of Nature that dance around us while we go about our human business in nature completely unaware.

Every flower, tree, mountain, river, ocean, and sea is teaming with a multitude of nature devas who overlight, support, nurture, and love them. In fact, your very own garden and house plants have an entourage of Light workers that is unique to them. When you talk to your plants, you are in fact, talking to the busy little 'worker bees' that are busily caring for their wellbeing. I like to think of these delightful little garden helpers as miniature Angels that happily flit about from plant to plant, like colorful hummingbirds on a divine mission.

In addition to the many elements of nature and the spirits of Nature, animals and humans are, of course, a large part of who occupies the astral plane. If you are a human with a pet, you understand fully that animals are a delightful part of Creation. Having their own sense of self, emotions, likes, and dislikes, our pets teach us that they, like humans, have a wonderful purpose on earth. Often times, our animal friends are a mirror to us, of the things in our lives that bring us great joy, and those places in our lives that need a little work. They are also some of the greatest teachers who have come into our lives to teach unconditional love.

Animals are particularly sensitive to Nature spirits and the spirits of those who have crossed over. Barking at what appears to be nothing, staring into what seems to be empty space, or running away from something that doesn't appear in physical form, are a few of the ways in which animals let us know we are not alone. And after all, no one has told them that it's just in their head or that their imagination has run away with them!

One evening, not long ago, I was awakened in the midst of a very deep sleep by the delightful sounds of laughter and giggling from what I perceived to be dozens of young children. Although I could not see them, I clearly heard their joy as it filled my bedroom from the other side of the veil.

Careful not to alarm my dogs, Merlin and Gabriel James, I laid quietly in my bed and enjoyed listening to the youthful voices that to me, began to sound like a flock of Angels.

With my children fast asleep in their bedrooms, and in accordance with the celestial voices increasing in volume and intensity, Merlin and Gabe popped up from their resting place at the foot of my bed and began to bark in the direction of the heavenly laughter that only the three of us could hear. Surprisingly, their barking and yapping did not deter our visitors from Spirit, nor did it wake Dane and Elyse.

Apparently understanding that there was no need to guard their territory, my furry little boys retreated from their defensive posture and with their heads cocking to the right and left in quizzical amusement, joined me in listening to the heavenly passersby.

We were mesmerized.

Following several captivating minutes in this state of otherworldly bliss, our divine visit from the realms of light and sound gently ended and my two little terriers fell fast asleep.

I was delighted to have the company of my little wizard and his brother the angel boy, to bask in such a delight with me. Their natural openness and innate knowing about their place in the wheel of life, makes them perfect companions on the Journey.

Humans on the other hand, can often be full of self doubt and ignorance about their place in the Natural scheme of things. From the well-trained masters of Light to those who walk in crowds of malfeasance, there are varying degrees of what I call "humans who have awakened."

From the moment that we are born, we begin the process of dying and the return to Home, which is Love. That pure, unconditional Love is sometimes called Light. As with all things that are finding their way Home, they look for signs along the way that tell them Home is somewhere near. The moment we take our first breath in human form, the search for Love, which is Home, begins.

Some humans are born into conditions and or families that have forgotten the True Source of their being. The remembrance of Home in the Love Light has faded from their collective memory. Humans who have not been helped to remember or have not yet embraced their Nature as a Child of Light, and the resplendent power of Love that comes with this acknowledgement, often try to find Love in all the wrong places.

There are those who believe that real power lies in the wielding of energies devoid of Light. Gossip, hatred, racism, bigotry, ignorance, violence, willful harm, manipulation … the list of offenses to our True Nature is long. These offenses belong to the realm of those who are, what I call, sleeping.

Ordinary people, living honest, ordinary lives are a beautiful lot. Not having heard the news that they are extraordinary, spiritual beings, often live a life giving their power over to unseen forces or persons that they feel possess 'special' powers or hold status over them. They do not yet realize that they are special too, and are gifted with numerous attributes and talents that the world is waiting for them to share.

For those that are generally aware that they have been given a gift of some sort, yet remain untrained, the journey of the adept is just around the corner. If however, they spend their lifetime without seeking further unfoldment and perfection of their Gifts, they are like a rosebud eternally frozen, forever waiting to blossom.

The one who chooses to fully awaken their Gifts, is the human who will begin the process of self realization and mastery. They will find and encounter numerous teachers during their lifetime to assist them in their spiritual development, while helping them to keep their eye on Love and their footsteps on the Path home to Light.

One of my favorite master teachers is the Coptic Master, Hamid Bey. During his lifetime as a prolific author, lecturer, and spiritual leader, he spoke much about the subject of self mastery and of becoming a Master. "A master is the one who is awake!" is perhaps my most beloved teaching from this wise Egyptian sage.

I believe that when we awaken from the slumber of an ordinary existence, our life becomes extraordinary and we cannot help but see that only Love and Light is real. To me, an awakened person sees that anything other than Love is an illusion that is brought to us as a form of sometimes painful learning that has the potential to help us find our true essence and safe passage Home.

Sometimes called the Initiations of Life, our trials and triumphs are Gifts that are given to us in order to help us master and balance our emotions, our thoughts, our perception of who we are, and to overcome our attachment to the material aspects of life. They are gifts that help set us free!

Humans that come to be known as Masters have done just this. They have overcome the trials of water, air, fire, and earth. By emancipating themselves from the fetters of third dimensional thinking, feeling, understanding, and attachments, they ascended into the realization of their true, solar Nature.

The physical presence of human beings on the astral plane is also complemented by the existence of non-physical human beings, those who have gone Home.

Ghosts, apparitions, spirits, spooks, specters, poltergeists, and the like, are names that we have chosen to give those who occupy the heavenly regions of the astral plane. Life without a physical body, finds those who have crossed over in their lightness of being. To varying degrees of course, depending on the details of your life, but all dancing about in what we deem the unseen astral world.

With the ability to step through the veil of the nonphysical into the physical, our loved ones who have gone Home are very much alive and loving. Like the Angels of Light, they are often messengers and guides who continue to love us from their place in the purity of Heaven.

On some occasions, our Angels of Light employ the aid and assistance of mortals to help them with their charges who are ensconced in a troublesome situation, even in the most exotic places on the astral plane:

A Case of Tomfoolery in the Valley of the Kings

If it's true that life is full of teachers and that we often learn through challenging times, the tomb of Thutmosis IV in the Valley of the Kings, Egypt proved to contain teachers, Angels, and unsuspecting rescuers of the most exceptional kind.

"Dana, beware of tomfoolery during your visit to Egypt." Thus began the conversation with my friend, Lisa.

She continued. "While you are there, dark forces are going to try and extinguish your life. Be cautious at all times and protect yourself. Promise me you will be on guard, Dana."

Responding to what I thought was simply an overly concerned friend, I said, "Of course I will, Lisa. Thank you for sharing your dream with me and for taking the time to call."

Five months after that conversation, I found myself in ancient Egypt. Specifically, I found myself, along with a dozen others in our travel group, standing in the magnificent Valley of the Kings. Like most foreigners who, for the first time, witness the vast expanse of the sand made mountain range that once contained the human relics and royal treasurers of the Pharaoh's, I was in awe.

Although the mummies and dynastic riches had long since been removed to museums, the fantastic hieroglyphic art depicting the story of their lives deaths, along with their mammoth sarcophaguses, still remained within each individual tomb.

While many in my group wished to see the tombs of King Tut, and Ramses IX, my soul longed to visit the tomb of Thutmosis IV, the 18th Dynasty ruler of Egypt, sometimes known as the Dreamer. My rational brain didn't have a reason as to why I would want to hike up the side of a steep mountain to visit the tomb of a pharaoh I knew little about. And yet, I asked permission of our Egyptian tour guide to do just that.

As I made my way up the steep mountain range lined with armed guards on camelback along its rim, I watched as two of my traveling companions, Laurie and Carlo Tonon from Sudbury, Ontario Canada, made their way to the outskirts far beyond the resting place of Thutmosis IV.

Before long, Laurie, a fourth degree black belt and Carlo, a sixth degree black belt and martial arts sensei were out of my sight.

Nearing the entrance to my destination, I was greeted by a friendly group of Italian travelers, who warned me that the descent into Thutmosis IV tomb was steep and trying. Wearing smiles of satisfaction upon their faces, members of the group assured me that I would enjoy the glorious hieroglyphics and the exquisite sarcophagus that awaited my arrival.

It was kind of them to warn me about the difficulties of maneuvering the tomb's interior terrain. Had they suspected, I am certain that they would have warned me about the life altering experience that was waiting for me as well.

Expecting to encounter a similar size group of travelers waiting to enter the crypt, I was surprised to find that I was the only person wishing to enter the pharaoh's grave. Handing my entry voucher to the assigned ticket taker, I was invited to step foot onto the descending platform, which would lead me down a vertical incline deep into the heart of the burial chamber of the Dreamer.

Cautiously and very aware of my footing, I began the downward journey into the dimly lit cavern. The colorful Egyptian hieroglyphs that adorned both sides of the narrow, stone-hewed corridor were, in some cases, still brilliantly clear and vibrant. The energy that surrounded me was both sacred and exciting. It was everything I had hoped to experience and soon I would realize, far more than I thought it would be.

With approximately one third of the downward climb behind me, I became aware of a hieroglyph I had not yet seen painted on any of the other temple antiquities. Directly to the right of me, was a large multihued bumble bee, a sign that would prove to be a portent of imminent danger.

Turning my gaze from the hieroglyphic harbinger hanging just above my shoulder, I focused once again on the steep downhill incline that was before me. Within a matter of seconds I could feel the presence of someone approaching me from behind. It was a physical presence that I was sensing and one that was determined to reach me in little to no time. A nudge to the upper portion of my back proved what my senses had been telling me, someone was on my heels and in a hurry to help me down the remainder of the platform steps.

Taking me by the arm, I was now being led downward by a man I did not know. His tall, gangly frame towered over my own. For a split second, I was rattled by fear.

In another instant, I heard my guardian Angel speak to me; "Dana, the ordeal that you now find yourself in is simply a test. The one who wishes to speak of and teach about the Angelic with authenticity, must experience the power and resourcefulness of the Angelis firsthand."

Simultaneously, my call for assistance to the Archangel St. Michael was already leaving the silence of my heart and mind; "Michael, Archangel of the 7th Heavenly Realm, I am calling to you. Please help me to see clearly what is going on here. Guide me in my words and decisions. Thank you for sending help to me!"

In what seemed like an eternity, but in reality was only a matter of minutes, I and my antagonist had reached the bottom of the Dreamer's tomb. In front of a sarcophagus dripping in the painted energy of the mother goddess Isis, we stood face to face.

Remembering what the Angels had moments before told me and staring directly into his onyx colored, almost lifeless eyes, I was the first to speak. "If you are an Angel of darkness who has come to challenge the veracity of my Light, you will not win. If you are an Angel of Light who has come to help me realize the fullness of my Light within, I am grateful."

Jerking me by the wrist, my adversary pulled me around and to the back of Thutmosis' antediluvian sarcophagus. With perhaps 3 feet of space between the massive granite coffin and the wall of the tomb, we were thrust together in what felt like a crypt of our own.

There was some part of me that felt great pity for the young man who had tightened his grip upon my arms. I couldn't help but wonder if he was a willing partner to this bit of mayhem, or someone who had been caught up on the spirit of something he knew little of.

"I know that you truly don't want to hurt me, do you?" I asked.

A few words in his native tongue fell from his lips as a miracle began to unfold just outside the entrance to the tomb.

The sounds of people rushing down the length of the stairs leading to Thutmosis' final resting place came closer. Frantic shouts in English and the sounds of the Egyptian ticket taker sounding a warning to my nemesis in Arabic, filled the descending corridor as my challenger once again grabbed me by the wrist in order to pull me away from the wall of the burial chamber and back out in front of the fully winged Isis.

Through a gentle mist of dust, I could see the faces of my Canadian friends, Laurie and Carlo. Without missing a beat or catching a breath, Carlo commanded both men to step away.

As Laurie stood in stunned silence, Carlo reached for my hand and boomed, "She is coming with us! Do you understand this?"

Both men nodded in the affirmative as Carlo and Laurie ushered me to the top of the tomb and out into the brilliant Egyptian sunlight.

Without looking back, the three of us made our way back down the side of the sandy foothill, until at last we came to a resting spot near the base of the Valley of the King's.

Clearly upset and with much concern for my safety, Carlo spoke in the most restrained manner he could muster, "My God, Denise, do you know what that man intended to do to you? Do you have any idea his intentions? That man wanted to end your life! Do you realize that? What in heaven's name were you doing there alone?"

My Angel team had obviously not spoken to Carlo's Angel team. Or, if they had, Carlo didn't get the message that the previous exercise in Angelic intervention had been just that; an exercise.

"It was just a test." That was my response.

"A test? What kind of a test are you talking about, Denise? That's one helluva test, my friend!"

Laurie and Carlo waited for my answer.

"Sometimes, life sends some pretty profound experiences to test us mere mortals. Trials by fire help us to understand the power of the Light and the power of that same Light that lives within us. The Light always wins. Today was another reminder of that unchanging fact."

Trying to lighten up the atmosphere, I continued, "When I knew that I was in trouble, I called out to the Archangel St. Michael and his legions of Light for help. And look, they sent the Canadian Mounties to my rescue!"

Not knowing whether to laugh or cry, both shook their heads in disbelief.

"How did you manage to find me?" I asked.

"We were clear on the other end of the valley, Laurie explained, when I sensed an urgency to leave the tomb that we were visiting. Without really knowing why, I told Carlo I wanted to visit the burial place of Thutmosis IV and he agreed. The closer we got to the entrance of the tomb, I could feel that something wasn't right. When we got right up to the door, one of the gentlemen at the entrance ran right past us, and began shouting as he made his way down the stairs. Carlo and I knew something was very wrong, so we followed him down into the crypt. We couldn't believe our eyes when we saw that young man pull you out to the front of the sarcophagus. I knew right then, why I had been feeling the way I had been. Thank goodness you're okay!"

Without further conversation, we made our way back to our traveling party. Each of us trying to digest the events that had just taken place, we spoke very little as the tour bus finally approached the waiting area.

Finding our seats within the safe confines of our motor coach, Carlo was the last one to enter. Without warning and with great exasperation, he exclaimed out loud, "I have never seen such tomfoolery in all my life!"

Stunned, I turned to look at him just as Laurie was replying, "Carlo, what did you just say?"

"I said," Carlo declared, "that I have never seen such tomfoolery in all of my life as I saw today in the Valley of the Kings!"

Laurie countered, "Carlo, where did you hear that word? I've never heard you use it before."

"Now that you mentioned it," he replied, "I really don't know. It just kind of flew out of my mouth. All I do know is that a glass of wine is in order tonight … maybe two!"

Earlier, I was convinced that Carlo's Angels hadn't clued him in to the events that were to unfold. In that instant, however, I knew that on some level, the message had indeed been received loud and clear.

The three of us spoke to very few people about what happened that day in the Valley of the Kings. To me, it was a profound lesson in the reality of Angelic intervention and the mighty bond of love that exists between those who inhabit the realm of heaven and the human beings that occupy earth.

It did, after all, send a couple of Canada's finest, dressed as black belt martial artists with a heart of gold; a pair of Light warriors who would become my lifetime friends.

Traveling to ancient Egypt has become a part of my life that I greatly enjoy. From her beautiful people and exotic terrain, to the prehistoric antiquities and relics of faith, it is a country and a people who are rich in history, love, and so much joy.

Let us now voyage across the celestial bridge of Light that leads us to what I call the Mental Plane and the Ocean of Light.

The Mental Plane
and the Ocean of Light

To the one who has awakened, the Ocean of Light provides beautiful glimpses into the realm of the Angels, the Elemental Kingdoms, and the Great Waves of color, Light, and sound. In their quest to explore, refine, and share their spiritual Gifts, the human who is on the road to self mastery learns to walk, talk, and listen to the occupants of this delicate realm.

Deep meditation and prayer are two of the ways that we can experience the Ocean of Light. Dream time also provides humans with a look into this realm. Whether we are fast asleep or find ourselves carried off into a wistful day dream, all of us are capable of being visited by or paying a visit to the upper realm of the Angelic during our dreams.

If you think of Angels as beings of pure Light, you're right. They are! If you believe that Angels come to us in the form or shimmering, colorful Light or in the sounds of celestial music playing in the silence of your mind, you are correct!

Angels who occupy the mental plane are divine messengers and yet very little is known about where they or their messages come from. Created from the elemental forces that emanate from the Universal Mind of God, these magnificent beings are in essence color, sound, and Light.

Thinking of the many planes of reality as radio frequencies, we can compare the Ocean of Light to a finer frequency than the astral plane, one that is made entirely of the purest elements of water, air, fire, and earth.

In an effort to help keep us on our true soul path, while experiencing the lessons of the earth plane, our Guardian Angels guide and guard us. By stepping down into a denser, astral form, or giving us a look into their own inherent state of existence within the mental plane, the Angels of Light who have been given charge over us are always trying to communicate with us.

Known for giving us splendid signs along the highway of life such as rainbows, miracles, visions, dreams, and divine synchronicities, they are able to enter our thoughts, prayer, and our meditation times in an effort to deliver their always loving message. They have been known to appear in animal form, musical form, and sometimes in the form of people that magically enter our lives.

Often, we meet up with the Angels of Light in a very sacred place called the Plane of Perfect Silence, where not even the sound of their gently flapping wings or the chords of their celestial tones may be heard.

The Plane of Perfect Silence

The monkey mind and the Plane of Perfect Silence are often at odds. That chatter filled center of doubt and busy-ness that overtakes our human mind is often the largest obstacle to sitting in the perfect Silence of the Heart and Mind of God.

Despite this human malady of monkey mind, our soul craves this amniotic state of Oneness. It is essential to our wellness that we take time to bathe in silence, though our feet are firmly planted in a state of endless astral chatter.

Saffron robes, mountain tops, fancy meditation benches, and cathedrals are not required in order to find this plane of stillness. Only a willingness to let go of your thoughts, your worries, your expectations, your doubts, your attachments, and your fears is required.

It is in this sacred act of the ultimate letting go, that we find the stillness of God within. Once found, we have made our way to The Plane of Freedom.

The Plane of Freedom

The pure silence of this plane speaks for itself.

As the master who has ascended beyond emotion, thought, ego, and the material world, we find ourselves in a state of luminous consciousness known as freedom.

"To lift your eyes to heaven
When all men's eyes are on the ground,
Is not easy.
To worship at the feet of the angels
When all men worship only fame and riches,
Is not easy.
But the most difficult of all
Is to think the thoughts of the angels,
To speak the words of the angels,
And to do as angels do."

-Essene Gospel of Peace

Chapter Three
The Mystic Angels

Creating the Mystic Angels Empowerment Deck began in the spring of 2009, as I worked to complete the manuscript for this book. At that time, the Angels of Light requested me to fashion a grouping of 33 cards, upon which their uplifting words of timeless wisdom would be recorded. While the messages of the Angels flow freely through me, the artistic endeavor would have to be the inspired work of another.

The Angels pointed me in the direction of the amazing talents of graphics artist, David Fix. Here is David's first hand account of our initial meeting to discuss the crafting of The Mystic Angels. It was a meeting that took place in the dreamscape:

"About July 1st, 2009, I dreamt that you and I were sitting facing each other lotus style near a stream at my childhood home on Squaw Lake. Birds were flying all around above us. I said to you earnestly, "I really want this to work. I want something magical to happen." You were whimsical and said nonchalantly, "Let's try this," and you took a magic wand and drew a bracelet of sparkles around my wrist and I started to float off the ground. I began flying around with the birds above. I was so *happy* I could hardly stand it, while you remained whimsical, unsurprised, and pleased."

Lots of love,
Dave

Using up to 20 separate photographs which were taken by David, each card has been individually crafted to express the Mystic Angels as they wished to be seen. As residents of the Higher Planes of Pure Light and Sound, the Angels appear to us in many forms. For those with eyes to see, ears to hear and a heart to feel, we find these Messengers of God, in all that we experience.

Each Mystic Angel delivers to you a single word to contemplate upon in the silence as you gaze at its figure. Within the Angelic portrait you will find an ancient esoteric symbol that helps to empower each card with ancient wisdom teachings. Following the message from the Angel, you will discover an uplifting and sacred mantra that you can recite to yourself throughout your day.

It is with great pleasure and with joyful hearts, that David and I, along with the Mystic Angels of Light, and our beloved editors, Sister Irene Mary and Eunice Norwood, present to you 33 Angelic encounters that have been designed to give you daily messages of love from the celestial realms and the Source of All Love.

In joy,
Dana

Archangel Azrael

Contemplative word: Power
Symbol: Scorpio the Mystic

The voice of your inner mystic is calling to you. Your guardian angel and guides in spirit are asking you to set aside a time of sacred silence each day. They lovingly invite you to pay attention to and trust the still, small voice of the Creator that whispers to you in meditation and prayer.

Daily mantra: "I am a wise and mighty spiritual being. I listen to the voice of my soul."

Archangel Barbiel

Contemplative word: Harmony
Symbol: Libra the Diplomat

Harmony and balance are the natural state of our soul. During the journey of life, this state of equilibrium can be overcome by confusion and pain. If there is an aspect of your life that is out of sync with your heart's true desire, or the calling of your soul, ask the radiant Archangel Barbiel to gently guide you along a sacred path that leads you back to harmonious living. Reclaim your state of joy!

Daily mantra: "I live in joyful Harmony with all of life."

Archangel Verchiel

Contemplative word: Open
Symbol: Leo the Governor of the Sun

You are a gloriously radiant Child of the Light! Archangel Verchiel asks you to cast aside any self doubt and relinquish all of your fears, as you step out on to the center stage of life. Lights, camera, action! Spirit is calling you to share your gifts and talents and claim your place in the sun.

Daily mantra: "I open my heart and mind to the loving warmth of the Sun. I am ready to shine!"

Archangel Hamaliel

Contemplative word: Compassion
Symbol: Virgo the Pure of Heart

Has anyone ever told you how much you are loved? Or, that nothing you have done in the past or ever will do in the future can separate you from the love of the Creator? Archangel Hamaliel reminds you that the One who created you, loves you without condition. This loving Angel of compassion asks that you give yourself this same gift of unconditional love.

Daily mantra: "My heart is a vessel of compassion toward all living things. I love myself."

Angel Phoenix

Contemplative word: Renewal
Symbol: Ankh the Key of Life

Every sunset heralds a glorious sunrise. And each of our days is a gift from the Universe, with a tag that reads:

> To: My Beloved
> Open with eagerness and great, dancing joy. Endless opportunities for happiness are contained within."
> *With love*: Your Maker

The Angel Phoenix helps you celebrate your spiritual growth and invites you to look ahead to the beauty that awaits your embrace.

Daily mantra: "Every moment of my life is an opportunity to begin again."

Angel Thoth

Contemplative word: Alchemy
Symbol: The Hermetic Caduceus

A healthy mind and spirit helps to create a healthy body and balanced existence. The Angel Thoth asks you to pay attention to the thoughts, foods, beverages and situations that you allow to enter your life. Give yourself the gift of loving words, healthy foods, and nourishing relationships that will magically create a life of wholeness that is part of your divine design.

Daily mantra: "I am whole and healthy. I set stable boundaries and allow the flow of loving thoughts to enter my mind."

Angel Yehudiah

Contemplative word: Birth
Symbol: The Great Pyramid of Giza

The Angel Yehudiah is here to help you celebrate your life! This splendid Angel of Light, wishes you to know how very much your life positively impacts others. Your service to the Light is recognized and honored by your Angelic guides and by the One who loves you most of all. You make a glorious and joyful difference in the world, and you are loved.

Daily mantra: "On this day, I honor my birth and my purpose for being, which is love."

Archangel Barchiel

Contemplative word: Creation
Symbol: The Spirit of Pisces

It is in the process of creating the life of our fondest dreams that we experience life.

Archangel Barchiel asks you to take his celestial hand in yours as you move forward into a radiant new phase of your life. Honor the past, live in the present, and welcome the wonderful adventures that are yours to be had. And don't forget to sing and dance along the way.

Daily mantra: "Together, Spirit and I create the life of my fondest dreams."

Archangel Ambriel

Contemplative word: Adapt
Symbol: The Gemini Mirror

When we can gaze into the mirror of another's eyes and see the face of God staring back at us, we understand the Great Mirror. When we can look upon the face of all of creation and see the love of our Maker dwelling there, we have become one with the Mirror.

Archangel Ambriel has come to acknowledge your ability to see the Oneness in All. With this great gift that you possess, you have come to earth to help heal the world. Blessing be upon you, wise one.

Daily mantra: "When I look in the mirror, I see the reflection of the Creator gazing back at me."

Archangel Jophiel

Contemplative word: Ecstasy
Symbol: Hindu

Ecstasy is perfect union. Delight in the one that we love or the One who loves us most of all, brings loving perfection.

Knowing that you are perfect in your imperfection should remind you, Dear One, that your life is indeed a journey of ecstatic oneness, a product of joy, a sign that Architect of the Universe was hopelessly, madly in love when you were fashioned and formed in Its glorious image.

Daily mantra: "God and I are one."

Angel Shamshiel

Contemplative word: Freedom
Symbol: Shinto

On the day you were born the stars danced with delight and the planets of the Universe jumped for joy!

The Angel Shamshiel comes to remind you that you are free to choose how you live, and that your life is a reflection of the choices that you make. Choose laughter, abundance, health, and endless love. Choose to sing from the mountain tops and dance with blissful abandon!

Daily mantra: "I am free to dance."

Archangel Blandine

Contemplative word: Enlightenment
Symbol: Buddhism

The mystics of old have taught us that a wise person realizes the impotence of gold and therefore invests in the currency of love.

Archangel Blandine encourages us to embrace a simpler way of life that unfetters us from the illusion that happiness can be found in material things. Take a walk, sit outdoors, converse with family, or make new friends. Plant a garden, sing your song, or simply choose to be. Be free!

Daily mantra: "I am free from all earthly desire. I am free."

Archangel Asariel

Contemplative word: Reflect
Symbol: Capricorn and the Mansions of the Moon

Every step along the Journey of Life gathers to us the experiences, people, places, and things that help to create our own unique story. This story becomes like a room filled with treasures within the Mansions of the Moon. Treasure, in the eye of the beholder, is glorious indeed. Since the dawn of time, you have been a priceless treasure in the eye of the One who beholds you. Share your story.

Daily mantra: "Every moment of my life has made me the beautiful Light that I have become."

Archangel Amethyst

Contemplative word: Precious
Symbol: Bahai

All of Creation is alive with the energies of the Universal Life Force of Love. Archangel Amethyst invites you to explore the exciting world of crystals and stone energies, who sing with a voice uniquely their own.

Known to help with meditation, balance, health, and insight, these beings of the earth and stars are calling you to investigate your relationship to them and how they might enhance your mystic journey.

Daily mantra: "I am a precious gem in the heart of Creation."

Wakinyan

Contemplative word: Growth
Symbol: The Medicine Wheel

The ancient Angelic form known as the Wakinyan or Thunderbeing prompts you to remember that life is a wondrous circle, in which all things are passing and yet, have always been and will always be. In the sacred hoop of life, every living thing is our brother and our sister. The Wakinyan thanks you for honoring all life forms and for walking gently upon Grandmother Earth. You are a beautiful spoke in the glorious medicine wheel of Life. We are One.

Daily mantra: "I am one with All in the Sacred Hoop of Life."

Archangel Chamuel

Contemplative word: Love
Symbol: Christ Light

Wherever there is an empty place, invite love to dwell within it. The Archangel Chamuel has come to remind you that love is your birthright; and a fact of who you are. It is time to gently love yourself and release anything from your life that no longer serves you in a loving way.

In order for love to finds its way into your life, there must be room for it to enter. Ask Chamuel to help you jettison the baggage of all that is unloving and useless, as you welcome more love into your life.

Daily mantra: "I am a living expression of the eternal Light of Love. I welcome love into my life."

Archangel Anael

Contemplative word: Light
Symbol: Isis the Star of Love

Your essence is Light. There are no greater or less than you.

The Archangel Anael is at your side asking you to further explore the vast expanse of your cosmic being through astrology and astronomy. Learning more about the astrological aspects of your birth, you see how the particles of stardust contained therein, participate in the dance of your existence. Study the cosmos and you are studying the inner workings of your very soul. Sit under a canopy of stars and gaze into the history of your Life.

Daily mantra: "My essence is Light. I am what the stars are made of."

Archangel Iahmel

Contemplative word: Change
Symbol: Air

The Net of Love is a constant companion to change. When we leap, it spreads gently below us, offering a safe harbor in which to land and grow.

Archangel Iahmel reminds you to breathe and to relax into each moment of your life. By embracing and moving through the many seasons of your life, you welcome the growth that comes with change. Rather than looking behind you or too far ahead, be in the season that is directly before you, loving the seasons yet to come.

Daily mantra: "I embrace change, knowing that my life is divinely guided."

Archangel Camael

Contemplative word: Confident
Symbol: Aries the Assertive

Be confident in who you are and in your ability to decide the course of your own life. You did not come to the earth plane to experience any form of servitude to the vision of life that others have for you.

The Archangel Camael comes to help you remember that the goals and dreams that you have set for yourself are enthusiastically supported by the Universe, your guardian Angel, and your guides in Spirit. They believe in you and the beauty of your dreams. Go for it!

Daily mantra: "I am supported by the Universe."

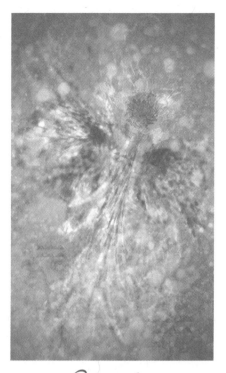

Archangel Cassiel

Contemplative word: Wealth
Symbol: Aquarius the Water Carrier

Wealth is measured by the one who receives a plenty.

The Archangel Cassiel brings to you a message of beauteous bounty. Whether it is a plenitude of health, happiness, contentment, love, money or adventure you seek, this Aquarian Angel will help you claim it. By asking her to lead you to this place of plenitude, you must be open to the way in which the Universe will respond in kind. Your preconceived notions and predetermined outcomes needs not come along for this ride. It's time to let go of the steering wheel and go along for an abundant ride with Joy.

Daily mantra: "Abundance is having a sufficiency for every moment of my life."

Archangel Advachiel

Contemplative word: Hope
Symbol: Sagittarius the Optimist

If hope springs eternal, then most certainly it sprang from the very same fount as that of your timeless soul.

The Archangel Advachiel teaches us that there is no room for doubt in the heart and mind of the one who realizes that with every storm comes a rainbow, with every ending a fresh beginning, with every heartbreak a new love is found. Advachiel thanks you for being the voice of hope for others and for understanding that sunrises are the results of sunsets. A beautiful sunrise is on your horizon.

Daily mantra: "I embrace each moment of my life, knowing that Love surrounds me."

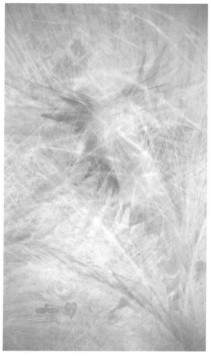

Archangel St. Gabriel

Contemplative word: Divine
Symbol: Water

The next time fear attempts to overshadow your hope, dash your heart's desire, expunge your joy or snuff out your Light, call upon the Archangel St. Gabriel, who will help you see that fear is the absence of trust in Spirit.

Always swimming in the waters of Spirit, the current of Love called Creator carries us to the realization of our Joy, our Purpose, our Love and our Source. Flow with life, knowing that anything less than loving is the illusion known as fear. Go with the flow.

Daily mantra: "I am a Divine child of God. Fear has no place with me."

Archangel Ariel

Contemplative word: Unity
Symbol: Earth

Gaia, our Earth Mother is a most glorious Angel. She supports us, feeds us, shelters us, and nurtures us in the splendor of her majestic mountains, rolling prairies, magnificent deserts, her endless oceans, rivers, and seas.

Archangel Ariel comes to tell you that Gaia is calling you to a closer connection with Her. By planting a garden, walking barefoot upon her sandy shores or grassy skin, you will hear the Earth Mother speaking to you. By swimming in her bodies of water, she will hold you gently while singing the Mother's song. Gaia beckons you to Her school of earthly learning. The playground awaits!

Daily mantra: "I am one with all of nature. I am one with Mother Earth."

Archangel St. Michael

Contemplative word: Triumph
Symbol: The Star of David

The lesson of the ascending and descending pyramid, known as the merkabah, is a message of perfect balance between earth and sky.

Archangel St. Michael tells us that the initiate who masters earth and sky, spirit and matter, body and mind, themselves becomes a true master. Taking the time each day to focus on your diet, meditation, prayer, and exercise, will help you triumph over the lessons that heaven and earth present to us in the form of obstacles.

Daily mantra: "I celebrate the lessons that I have learned in my life. I rejoice in what they have taught me."

Archangel Metatron

Contemplative word: Transformation
Symbol: Tree of Life

Like a butterfly being called from its shimmering cocoon, your Higher Presence is calling you to the next phase of learning along your soul's journey.

The Archangel Metatron will see to it that the proper teachers, books, workshops, and tele-classes are brought to your attention in the coming weeks, as you stretch your spiritual wings and your Higher mind toward the wisdom teachings of the ancients. This is a time for advanced esoteric learning.

Daily mantra: "I Am that I Am."

Archangel Selaphiel

Contemplative word: Prayer
Symbol: Hathor the Loving Mother

The Archangel Selaphiel joyfully reminds you that every thought that you think, every word that you speak, becomes a sacred prayer in the Universal web of interconnectedness. As the Light Angel of Prayer, Selaphiel thanks you for those times that you have made prayers on behalf of another and for those times that you have been the answer to a prayer for someone in need. You, your life, and your purpose as a Light bearer, are a prayer in expression upon the Earth plane.

Daily mantra: "My thoughts are prayers. Let them be loving and kind."

Archangel St. Raphael

Contemplative word: Healing
Symbolism: The Dove of Peace

The peace that you seek is at hand, and within. The healing that you wish for is to be found in the peace of knowing that only Love is real and to that Love you will one day return.

The Archangel St. Raphael, sometimes known as the healer of those gone blind, has come to open your eyes to the beauty that lies within you and all around you. This glorious Angel of Healing asks that you spend time with him each day in the silence of your heart to receive the healing vibration of his presence. Give to Raphael anything that makes you feel less than whole, and let this mighty Archangel fill you with peace.

Daily mantra: "Peace is within me. I am at peace."

Angel Nathaniel

Contemplative word: Joy
Symbol: Fire

Joy is a state of Grace. It is the art of being in love with your life; and all aspects and experiences of your life. It is the understanding that your unique existence is like a splendid thread of silk that is continuously weaving itself into the Magic Carpet of Life.

The Angel Nathaniel asks you to join him on the Magic Carpet and to fall in love with yourself and your life, once again.

Daily mantra: "I am fired up about life and joyful in my existence."

Archangel Muriel

Contemplative word: Balance
Symbol: Cancer the Sensitive

By walking in balance between heaven and earth, the best of both worlds become our reality.

The Archangel Muriel has come to tell you that you are a wonderfully sensitive, intuitive, and loving being. She asks you to embrace your psychic self by paying attention to the promptings of your Angels and Guides. Muriel reminds you that signs from Spirit are all around, and that those we have loved, who have gone Home to Heaven, are always near.

You are loved.

Daily mantra: "I am in balance with Life. I am strong, sensitive, and wise."

Archangel Asmodel

Contemplative word: Patience
Symbol: Taurus the Steadfast

Divine timing is a matter of understanding that you are Divine and that your Higher Self and the Architect of Life have agreed to determine the perfect timing of the events in your life.

The Archangel Asmodel, would like you to know that you are on the right Path. Be prepared for doors to unlock and windows to open, with this steadfast Angel of Light at your side. Keep moving forward, one step … or one leap of faith at a time.

Daily mantra: "All things happen in Divine timing. I live in the present moment."

Archangel St. Uriel

Contemplative word: Forgiveness
Symbol: Christianity

In the instant that you forgive yourself or another, you have selflessly given the precious gift of unconditional love. In the moment that you love yourself in your perfect imperfection, you have given yourself permission to love on the deepest of levels.

Remember, release, forgive and embrace your Love.

Daily mantra: "I forgive myself and others by forever giving love. I love my perfect imperfection."

Archangel Raziel

Contemplative word: Shine
Symbol: The Flower of Life

Blessed Being of Light Supreme,

You have been created to brilliantly, lovingly, joyfully, shine! As the sunflower blooms to stand tall upon the plane of earth, you too have been called to stand radiantly within the presence of your Higher Power and to cast the seeds of your Light upon the fertile soil in the garden of life.

With your back to the shadow and your face to the Sun, Archangel Raziel has come to help you plant the seeds of your heart's desire, water them tenderly with prayer and watch them unfold into dreams come true. It is time to bring your hopes and dreams to life.

Daily mantra: "I am the Light of the Divine, forever blooming, and always loving."

Archangel St. Israfel

Contemplative word: Awaken
Symbol: Islam

A wise Coptic Master once said, "A master is the one who is awake!"

The Archangel St. Israfel has come to help you awaken from your slumber. For you, there will be no more hiding under a bushel basket or hibernating within the confines of your self imposed comfort zone. It is time for you to see the magnificent Gifts that you hold and to share those precious gems with the world around you. Paint, write, create, dance, speak, chant, build, love, encourage, counsel … sing the unique song of your soul!

Daily mantra: "I am alive. I am awake. I am that I am."

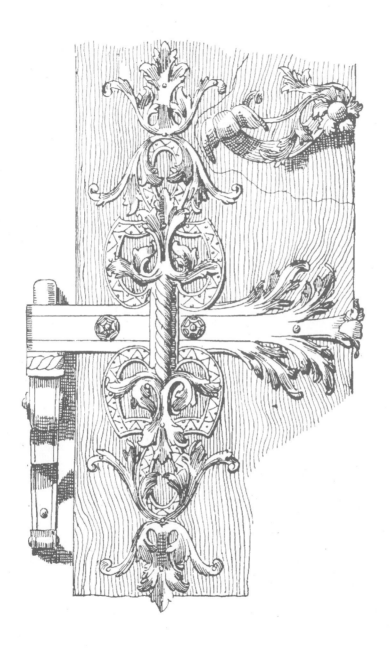

Every Child

Has known God,

Not the God of names,

Not the God of don'ts,

Not the God who ever does

Anything weird,

But the God who only knows four words

And keeps repeating them saying:

"Come dance with Me."

Come

Dance.

-Hafiz, Sufi Master
From "The Gift"

Chapter Four
A Year of Affirmations

Love Letters from the Angels

hroughout the course of writing this book, the Angelis graciously gifted me with dozens of love letters. These epistles of loving kindness and wisdom are contained in the pages that follow.

Read them as though they were written especially for you. They were.

You may wish to let your Angels help you randomly choose a single letter to read upon waking in the morning or prior to resting at night. By closing your eyes and asking them to guide you, the Angels will bring you to the perfect love letter for a particular moment in time.

Contemplate them, take them into meditation or share them with those you treasure and those in need of loving encouragement. Everyone can use a compassionate pick me up from the Heavens.

Let's begin by dancing with the Archangel Azrael …

"Dance"

Dance with the Light* Blessed One,
Dance!
Dance with the Spirit of Love, letting your Heart take the lead.
Dance with the Spirit of Oneness, letting your Eyes lead the way.
Dance with the Spirit of Healing, letting your Hands guide the flow.
Dance with the Spirit of Growth, letting your Legs forward march.
Dance with the Spirit of Understanding, letting your Ears hear the Truth.
Dance with the Light* of Forever, letting your inner Temple Shine forth.
Dance with the Light* of Laughter, letting your child within take your hand.
Dance with the Light* of your Guardian Angels, letting them open miraculous doors.
Dance with the Light* of the Past, Present, and Future, knowing that the Now contains them all.
Dance with the Light* of Hope, letting fearlessness lead each step.
Dance the Dream of Love, BeLoved, where there truly is no missed step.
All is in perfect order, all is well.
Your dancing shoes await you,

Archangel Azrael
Celestial Dance Instructor

"Shine"

Brothers and Sistars of Light,

When we ask that you "Let your Light Shine," we are speaking of the radiance of the Divine Flame of Life that is encased within and entrusted to each of you.

When you call upon the assistance of the Angelic Realm, we ask that you harken upon the Angelic Guardians of Light, who are here to assist in the vibratory ascension of the Earthly Mother and all living Beings who dwell upon Her.

It is time to bring Heaven to Earth.

By calling upon the Guardians of Light without, you are by decree, calling upon the Guardian of Light forces within you.

As you Shine, the night sky is illumined, without and within.

Shine an open heart.

Shine an open mind.

Shine with open arms.

Shine a purpose filled stride.

Shine your Dreams of Peace.

Shine your Hopes of Joy.

Shine your Dance of Laughter.

Shine with an outstretched hand.

Shine with your voice of reason.

Shine without expectation of thanks.

Shine because it is who you are, to do so.

Hold up your Candle. Light up your world!

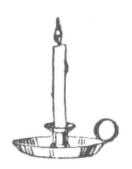

Luminous Love,
Archangel Jophiel

"Feed the World"

Beloved farmer of Celestial Light Supreme,

The world is hungry for Light*
It is time to take up your hoe and feed the world!
As you till the soil of each new day, remember to plant rows of Peace, Joy, Love, Learning, Ascension, Health, and Playfulness.

With each Light* seed of Peace, shall peace return 100 fold.

With each Light* seed of Joy, shall joy return 100 fold.

With each Light* seed of unconditional Love, shall unconditional love return 100 fold.

With each Light* seed of Learning, shall learning return 100 fold.

With each Light* seed of Ascension, shall ascension return 100 fold.

With each Light* seed of Health, shall health return 100 fold.

With each Light* seed of Playfulness, shall playfulness return 100 fold.

When you feed the hungry, you nourish yourself.
Plant, nurture, harvest, and enjoy the fruits of your Light* labor.

In gratitude for your selfless service,
Archangel Ariel

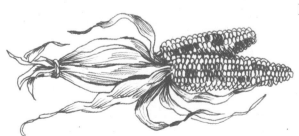

"Angels on Earth"

Beloved Light*worker,

Blessed are the Peace.makers
        ...they are Angels of Respite on Earth.

Blessed are the Love.makers
        ...they are Angels of Compassion on Earth.

Blessed are the Joy.makers
        ...they are the Angels of Heaven on Earth.

Blessed are the Trust.makers
        ...they are the Angels of Comfort on Earth.

Blessed are the Wholeness.makers
        ...they are the Angels of Healing on Earth.

Blessed are the Balance.makers
        ...they are the Angels of Justice on Earth.

Blessed are the Friendship.makers
        ...they are the Angels of Happiness on Earth.

Blessed are the Trouble.makers
        ...they are the Angels of Integrity Testing on Earth.

Blessed are the Vision.makers
        ...they are the Angels of Clear Sight on Earth.

Blessed are the Angels cloaked in flesh and bones
        ...they are emissaries of Light* on Earth.

I Am,

                Archangel Sandalphon
        The Prophet of Ascending Angels on Earth

"Awareness"

Greetings of Great Awareness!

Awareness that **your** unique and splendid Light* of peacefulness is needed upon the Earth Mother at this time.

Awareness that through mastery of the Self, your Light* shines ever brighter throughout the vast expanse of the unending cosmos.

Awareness that those who awaken to their true nature ... are Masters of the One Light*.

Awareness that your unique, eternal Light* is guiding the further unfoldment and expansion of the Divine Light* Matrix.

Awareness that no amount of darkness can extinguish Light*.

Awareness that no amount of hatred can extinguish, Love.

Awareness that YOU are awakening to your True nature as a Master of Divine Light* within the Matrix of Love ... that expands as your soul expands, in the remembrance that *no* amount of darkness can extinguish your Light* and no amount of hatred can extinguish your Love.

Be aware Beloved, that you are dancing upon the Divine Light* Matrix of Love, as a joyful, Living Light* of the Creator in expression.

Dance the joy.full dance of Light* eternal.

And so it is,

St. Uriel
The Fire of God

"Love Your.self"

Beloved Child of Peacefulness,

As you love your.self, you love all others.

As you heal your.self, you heal another.

As you forgive your.self, you forever give to another.

As you smile at your.self, others smile in return.

As you give to your.self, others receive your gift.

As you continue to explore, others benefit from your travels.

As you expand your library of conscious knowledge, others learn with you.

As you learn to laugh at your.self, others will see the joys within.

As you remember your Light*, others will shine brightly, too.

As you embrace the One within, everything with.out becomes the One.

As you look upon the stars in the heavens, the stars within rejoice.

As you bask in the Sun, the Sun radiates through you.

And so it is, in the Web of Love.

Archangel Sandalphon

"As Above, So Below"

Blessed Beings of Light Supreme,

In the sacred space of Now, recite each word to yourself and feel the emanation of the angelic essence of each:

*Day.Light
*Moon.Light
*Sun.Light
*Heart.Light
*Love.Light
*Inner.Light
*Red Light
*Orange Light
*Yellow Light
*Green Light
*Blue Light
*Indigo Light
*Gold Light
*Rainbow Light
*Angel Light
*Healing Light
*One Light
*Light

And breathe …

As above, so below.
As without, so within.

And breathe …

St. Raphael
Archangel of Clear Sight

"The Holidays"

Blessings of the Holy Days to you ... Holy One.

Honoring the blessed Holiness of you, I AM.

From the Breath, Love, and Light* of the Holy Oneness did you emanate in perfect Angelic form, complete.

From your birthplace of Light* did you choose to descend into form, to become the Light* of a darkened world.

"Let there be Light!" said the One.

And you became.

From the Point of Holy Light did All begin. That Point of Holy Light is you.

Let your Holy Light* Shine before all others so that they might remember their Divine Radiance and see the Path of Love that exists in the Holiness of Now.

All time is now. All Light* is Now. All Love is now.

The time to shine your Light* of Love is Now.

I AM

In Awe of Your Light,
Gabrielle, Archangel of Announcements and Light*

"Power Within"

Blessings of the Brightest Light* Beloved,

We, of the Angelic Realm of Pure Light and Pure Sound, wish to remind you of the tremendous power that lies within you.

The power to Laugh
The power to Scorn
The power to Love
The power to Hate
The power to Heal
The power to Harm
The power to Uplift
The power to Tear Down
The power to Know
The power to Ignore
The power to Create
The power to Destroy
The power of Light*
The power of Shadow

The Power to CHOOSE the Power that You Wield!

Choose to Laugh, to Love, to Heal, to Uplift, to Know, to Create in the Light* of Who You Are...

The Creator of Angels in expression.

St. Michael
Archangel of the Sword of Light

"The Dawn"

Be.Loved,

The glorious breaking of Dawn, heralds the awakening of a new Day...which heralds a gentle Dusk .... followed by the setting of the Sun... which heralds the glorious breaking of Dawn...

And so it has always been...and so you shall always be...Gloriously Dawning, Awakening, Settling, Setting, and Rising once again...like the Sun*

Rise! Awaken! Shine! ... Settle, Set, and Rise once more!

"All is well, and all manner of things are well."

In the Light* of the Sun,
Uriel, Archangel

"Glorious Light of Love"

Loving Child,

Glory Be said the Great I AM
Glory Be.came You

Let there Be Light* said the Great I AM
Light* Be.came You

Let there Be Love said the Great I AM
Love Be.came You

Glorious Light of Love

In the darkest places, Be the Glorious Light of Love
In the lightest places, Be the Glorious Light of Love

In sorrowful places, Be the Glorious Light of Love
In joyful places, Be the Glorious Light of Love

In the fearful places, Be the Glorious Light of Love
In the empowered places, Be the Glorious Light of Love

In the ignorant places, Be the Glorious Light of Love
in the learned places, Be the Glorious Light of Love

In the hateful places, Be the Glorious Light of Love
In the loving places, Be the Glorious Light of Love

Be all that you came to be ... Glorious Light of Love

Beauty full

In Love's Glorious Light,
Archangel St. Raphael

"Angel of the Air"

Child of Beauty,

Bright Blessed Beauty...

Bright Blessed Beauty of You,

Angel of the Air - The Angel of Friday, Am I.

Breathing deeply, repeat after me:

"Angel of the Air, enter my lungs and fill my entire body with the Light* of Life!"

"Angel of the Air, enter my lungs so that I might breathe the Love of Life!"

"Angel of the Air, enter my lungs so that I might speak the Words of Light*"

"Angel of the Air, enter my lungs so that I might feel you dancing in my Heart!"

"Angel of the Air, gently waft your Heavenly scent upon and within me, so that I might become a vehicle for the Light* of Life"

And so it is.

The Angel of the Air
Friday

"In the Beginning"

Bright Star Blessings to All Who Read These Words
and to those with whom these words are shared...

In the Beginning,
all Things emanated Angelic Light*

In the Beginning,
were you.

In the End,
All Things Angelic return to the One Home.

In the End,
The One Home is where you shall return.

Between the Beginning and the End,
you are asked to Play ... to Dance ... to Sing ... to make a Joyful noise.

Between the Beginning and the End,
you are asked to share your unique Light* Emanation with the world.

The Stars Above,
reflect your radiant Star within.
Shine, like the vast expanse of the Cosmos!

The Sun Above,
shines warmly and brightly in you.
Radiate the warmth of the Creator like never before!

The Moon Above,
glows like the ancient wisdom you contain.
Share your knowledge with the world!

In the Beginning...emanated all things Angelic, who came to earth to play, to sing, to dance and to make a joyful noise. They came to share their unique Light* with all of creation, shining like the Sun, reflecting like Stars and glowing like the moon...before returning to the One Home, where joyful homecoming celebrations are had and golden badges of courage are bestowed, by those Angelic Emanations who have gone before and those who hope for the privilege to one day go.

In the beginning, in between, and in the end ... are you.

St. Israfel
Archangel of the Hero's Journey

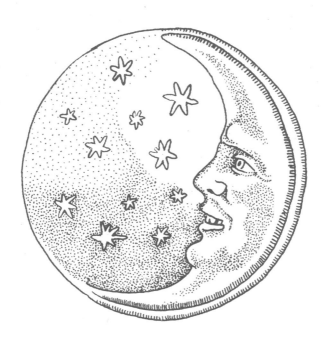

"Shine Like the Sun"

Bright Beautiful Child of the One Shining Sun,

This is Archangel Uriel, "He Who Shines Like the Sun."
I come this day to tell you, that like my Essence, you too, "Shine Like the Sun."
"Shine like the sun?" you ask.

In.deed you do!

Each time you feed the hungry Spirit of another, you shine*
Each time you clothe another in your unconditional love, you shine*
Each time you shelter another in the warmth of your smile, you shine*
Each time you uplift another with a loving hand, you shine*
Each time you wipe a tear and replace it with a warm embrace, you shine*
Each time you replace doubt with words of faith, you shine*
Each time you help the blind to see the Light Within them, you shine*
In the days of old, the Priest King of Atlantis would begin each day, "Let the Light Shine!"
In the days of the Pharaohs Dispensation, they would begin each day, "Let the Light Shine!"
In the endless days of All Time, we say, "Let the Light Shine!"
Many times, we of the Angelic Realm have come to you, unaware!

When I was hungry, when I was naked, when I was homeless, when I was sick, when I was lonely, when I was doubtful, when I was fearful...

You let your Light* shine!

In the Light of the One Who Sees All,
Archangel Uriel

"The Grand Dream"

Blessings of this Glory.us Day Precious Beings of Sun Light,

I Am the one known as Sandalphon!
My message today is one to help cheer you on.
Just as I ascended, so shall you.
Just as I realized my Angelic beingness, you shall too.
Just as I ascended into the Realization that Angels all are we,
I came to discover the true essence of Me.
In the beginning... all things emanated Angelic from the Source of the Sun,
Together... Angels, Source, Creator, Love, and Sun...we are One.

Focus on the beating of your Beloved Heart and feel it join in the Universal Rhythm
of the Life Stream ~

There...in the silent still point is where you enter the Grand Dream ~
Remembering when you chose to come Alive and Awake...
To serve the greatest good and to Love for One another's sake.
The Dreamer has awakened, the Dreamer is you.
Ascend...you have...knowing that the Dream you create is a reflection of You.
The Heights are yours, the Depths are too.
Remember, Angel - that only Love is true.

In Loving Service,
Archangel Sandalphon

"The One"

Blessings Beautiful You, One and All …

You who are the Creator in expression.

You who are part and parcel of the Divine Matrix of Life.

You who are given each moment to choose, how you will live that moment.

We ask that you live each moment in Joy.

When you are able to see the Joy through Less Than, you will have found your True Nature and the Song of the Matrix.

Joy is the Nature of the Song of the Loving Divine Matrix.

Less Than is **I**.llusion. **Ill**.usion.

Be unattached to Ill.usion. Let the Seer see its false Nature.

Let the Seer see the Truth.

When you, who are made in the image and loveliness of the One, are Joyful, the Matrix Light shines through you. Your brothers and sisters are gifted your living prayer of Joy, and ALL is well.

Joy is **well**.ness. **WE**.llness

Be joy.full. Be well.

All is well...

Archangel Raphael
Angel of We.llness

 *"Shining One"*

Shining One,

Yes, **you**. You are a Shining One*

Made to shine like a thousand Suns through the Light of Day and the Darkness of Night.

Like a bumble bee landing on a radiant flower born of Spring.

Made to shine like a small child feeling its toes wiggle in the grass for the very first time.

Like the sound of Joy through the sadness of Pain.

Made to shine like a diamond, who has risen from the womb of Mother Earth.

Like the feeling of Love through the emptiness of Loss.

Made to stretch like the gentle lotus blossom, having been birthed from the water and soil.

Like the vision of Splendor through the path of Destruction.

Made to sing like the birds at Dawn.

Made to LIVE...fully..wondrously...joyously... aware that only LOVE is real.

Only the Light* of Love is real.

You are Real.

In Love,
St. Raphael, Archangel

"2012"

Human Beings of Light,

Do not become discouraged by those who would say that the world is coming to an end, or those who would say that cataclysmic events are going to alter the world of Gaia.

They do not understand that it is the inner world that is dying in each, to make room for a brand new, beautiful, loving, Aquarian world within!

They do not understand that loving, cataclysmic events are altering the world within each, to create a world of Oneness with All.

It's time for "out with the old, and in with the New!"

All those in favor...time to jettison the 'baggage' and prepare for wondrous flight.

Keep steady in the eye of the Aquarian storm, Be.loved.

Aquarius is not about "I" it's about "us". Aquari.us.

"Let the sun shine in..."

Archangel Uriel
"The Fire of the Creator"

"Child of Light"

Beloved,

Breathe deeply the Infinite Intelligence contained within the Air...
        Exhale the Radiance of Light*

Breathe deeply the Infinite Intelligence contained within the Air...
        Exhale the Love of Light*

Breathe deeply the Infinite Intelligence contained within the Air...
        Exhale the Joy of Light*

Upon your head rests your Crown of Light Glory, feel it glowing...
        radiating your soul Light*

Imagine me.
See me.
Feel me.
Hear me.
Smell me.

The one known as Jophiel, Am I.
The one known as a Child of Light, are you.
Feel the Light Circuits in your bodies connect with the Light Circuits of the One*
Rest here.
Hold the Light.

Say to yourself...I am Love, I am Joy, I am abundance, I am song, I am eternal, I am wisdom, I am laughter, I am dance, I am poetry, I am nature, I am my brother, I am my sister, I am Light, I am all that ever was, All that is, All that ever will be.

And so, you are.

In Love,
St. Jophiel, Archangel

"Spend Time Outdoors"

Beloved,

On this day of Harmonic Beauty...take your physical vehicle, the body, out into the Love Sounds and Light of Mother nature, for even a few moments.

Lift your face to the sun, drink in the wind and sun...synchronize your Heart to the Heart of the One*

Be filled with the magic and wonder of U*niverse

The Angelis Cosmos loves you

As do I...for all Eternity...

St. Michael,
Archangel of the 7th Heaven

"The Knight"

Beloved,

When you find yourself dancing with the Dark Knight, rest in the knowledge that the Light* of Day greets you at the coming Dawn*

Though the dance with the Knight may be slow and painful, seemingly never to end, the dancer learns in the process to glide fluidly through the waltz of Life, recognizing that each movement is necessary for the overall dance of the Soul.

Dancing in the Light* of Day becomes a Joy of Glorious proportions when one has completed the Dance through Darkness with the Knight of Initiation.

Dance, Be.Loved.

Dance!

Boldly, Courageously, Joyously, and Lovingly Dance!

Archangel Theliel
Your Life Dance Instructor

"Just for Today"

Beloved,
Just for today...

Each time you begin to say something unkind to yourself, stop and repeat after me:

I am perfect in my imperfection.
I am Light*
I am learning
I love myself

Just for today...

Each time you begin to say something unkind about another, stop and repeat after me:

They are perfect in their imperfection
They are Light*
They are learning
I honor their Path

Shower blessings upon yourself and others ... and watch the rainbow bridges appear.

Archangel Milkiel

"*Open Your Eyes and See*"

Beloved Child of Light,

"You have always been."

"You will always be."

"The choice of Joy is yours."

"Open yours Eyes and see."

"You were not placed on Earth to merely exist."

"You were created and placed here to experience A Love and A Joy that is completely free."

"If only… you will open your Eyes, beloved."

"And See."

St. Raphael,
Archangel of Healing and Healers

"Conscious Dreamer"

Splendid Child of Light*,

Do not be afraid
Be Alive!

You are the Dreamer Awake
Consciously Dreaming a New Day into Being!

Remember Beloved...

Only Love is Real.
Anything other than Love is an Ill*usion
that you have come to unmask!

Reveal the Light

Remember Dear One...

The Seer lies behind the Eyes
Open your Eyes to Joy!

Awakened Dreamer
Dream Love into Being!

Do not be Afraid
Be Alive!

Dream well,

Archangel Theliel
Angelic Prince of Love

"Joyfully Aware"

Blessings of Joyful Awareness to All Who Read These Words and Feel the Presence of Light* Within

Beloved Children of the One Joy,

Be Joyfully aware that you are Power*full *

Be Joyfully aware that you are Beauty*full *

Be Joyfully aware that you are Peace*full *

Be Joyfully aware that you are Light*filled *

Be Joyfully aware that you are Love*filled *

Be Joyfully aware that you are Eternal Light*

Be Joyfully aware that you have always Been and will always Be *

Be Joyfully aware that you are Perfectly made *

Be Joyfully aware that your Uniqueness is Heaven in Creative Expression *

Be Joyfully aware that you are never, ever alone *

Be Joyfully aware that Earth is a School *

Be Joyfully aware that All is Well *

Be Joyfully aware that Heaven is Real *

Be Joyfully aware that Heaven is Within *

Be Joy

Give Joy

Sing Joy

Joy is found by those courageous Souls who understand that only Love is Real and that they themselves are that very Love, in eternal, joy.full motion

St. Israfel,
Archangel

"Imagine"

Be.loved,
Imagine...
for a moment...
that you are living the life you have always dreamed of.

Imagine that life.
Feel that life.
See that life.
Hear that life.
Smell that life.

Imagine...
That there are unseen helpers who have been given charge of helping you create the life you dream of.

Imagine...
That with a simple call for "help" and a willingness to "let go" and a heart of courage to "move forward" ...

You can experience a moment of joy, as you remember when you could only imagine, that your life could be all that your heart desires

Imagine...
What is the worst thing that can happen by taking the first step toward making your dream a reality?

*You may have to give up being and doing all things for all people
*You may have to let go of outdated belief systems
*You may have to begin loving yourself more and hurting for others less
*You may have to give up the control that you really do not have
*You may have to give up being angry, resentful, and depressed
*You may have to smile more as your dream becomes real

*You may have to say "thank you" to the Oneness for all of the abundance in your life
*You may have to say good-bye to feeling "less than"
*You may have to say hello to new friends
*You may have to let go of society's expectations
*You may have to banish fear and all things that have made you fearful, including people who have frightened you
*You may have to forgive yourself...and others
*You may have to buy new outfits
*You may get healthy
*You may get happy
*You may dance more
*You may learn more
*Your wings may unfurl
*You might take flight
*You may feel fulfilled
*You may wish you'd called for help sooner and taken the first step long ago....
Imagine...finding out...together.

Love,
Your Guardian Angel

"Peace"

Beloved Child of Peace,

Peace is the Light* from which All things emanate

Peace is the Light* that you carry within

Peace is the Love from which you were conceived

Peace is the Love to which you will one day return

Peace is the song that was sung in the womb

Peace is the song that you came to sing

Peace is the wisdom that you express with each breath

Peace is the wisdom that sees

Peace is the state of the Spirit who knows

Peace is our Home

Peace be with you

Peace be with*in you

Peace Be

You

Gabrielle,
Archangel of Peacefulness

"Change"

Blessings Beloved Beings of Light* Supreme,

I AM St. Michael, Archangel of Courage, Fortitude, and Heavenly Change.

Change is the constant inward flow of growth for those with eyes to see it as such.

See that Change is Growth!

Change is the vehicle for letting go, for those with a heart to understand it as such.

Understand that Change brings Freedom!

Change is the vehicle for giving yourself a new voice in the world, for those willing to sing a new song.

Know that Change Empowers!

Change is the Gift that allows us to re-create our reality, for those with a mind to understand it as such.

Know that you can Re-Create at any time!

Change allows us to release limiting beliefs, for those with a Spirit that wishes to expand.

Understand that you are Limitless!

Change allows you to look at things in a brand new way, for those willing to explore a different possibility.

Know that you are supported as you explore the vastness of your possible-abilities!

Let Go
Be Free
Sing a New Song
Empower Yourself
Re*Create
Release
Expand
Explore
Play
Let Your Light* Shine
Change...the vehicle of Love in Motion!

St. Michael,
Archangel of the 7th Heavenly Realm

"Trust"

Blessings of Divine Grace to all who read these words and to whom these words will be shared,

I Am Metatron.

Rainbow colored, like you, Am I.

The colors of the rainbow emanating from and within you... a Divine Reflection of the Rainbow Light Love from which you were born as a Thought in action.

TRUST is my Gift on this eve.

TRUST that you are precisely where you are supposed to be at this point in All of Time.

TRUST that you are perfection in your perceived imperfection.

TRUST that you are loved by the One who Loves you Most of All.

TRUST that your Heart is connected to the One Heart.

TRUST that your beauty is required and most needed on Earth at this magnificent time of great change.

TRUST that change is growth.

TRUST that you are never, ever, for one Moment alone.

TRUST that the Creator who loves you and is you, is superbly radiant within you

TRUST that Light always wins.

TRUST that you are Whole. The Universe is, after all, Whole.

TRUST that when you seem to fall, Love is here to pick you up.

TRUST that if you ask, you will be answered.

TRUST that if you knock, the door will be opened.

TRUST that darkness is an illusion.

TRUST that Light* is your Home.

TRUST that ALL things need Love.

TRUST that LOVE is available to all.

TRUST that your words are power*full. Speak them wisely.

TRUST that your thoughts create. Create only beauty.

TRUST that your intentions manifest. Manifest with love.

TRUST that what you do to One you do to yourself. Treat yourself well.

TRUST that I Am by your side.

In Loving Trust,
Metatron, Archangel Most High

"Timelessness"

Angel of the North - Prince of Majesty, Domiel is my Name.

Assisting you in seeing the Goodness and Glory in All things is my Heavenly task.

Just for today and hope-fully for tomorrow...slow down, stop for just a moment, and take a look around you.

In that sacred moment of timelessness, drink in the Goodness and Glory all around you, and give thanks.

Remember to breathe …

As you breathe in the goodness all around, you nourish your physical, spiritual, mental, and emotional bodies.

Just for today, and hope-fully for tomorrow...slow down, stop and embrace yourself.

In the timelessness of that sacred moment, drink in the Goodness and Glory of YOU, and give thanks.

Remember to breathe …

As you breathe in the Majesty, Grace-fullness, and Joy-fullness of YOU, you nourish your very Soul. You shine like the Sun.

You remember Who You Truly Are, Be-Loved One.

Let us breathe together, the Love of All that Is.

With Infinite Gratitude for Your Goodness and Glory,

Archangel Domiel
Angel of Heavenly Connections

"Speak Your Truth"

Blessings of this Wonder.Us Day, Beloved,

As leader of the Choirs of Heaven, my name is Jeduthun.

As director of Angelic Truths and Harmony, I lead you on the Path of Empowerment.

Together, we will empower you to take back your voice and to once again speak out when something is important to you! When you stop speaking your Truth, a small part of your Spirit recedes and becomes forgotten.

I Am here to re-mind you that...

You have been given a voice with which to bless the world with your unique, Splendid Song. The Heavens are now calling you to sing It once more.

On this very day, I ask you to find a place of quiet and to call upon me. At my arrival, I ask that you speak, hum, or sing out loud to the Universe...from your Heart...to the Heart of the Creator.

Sing your song loudly, beautifully and in a way that only YOU can!

Sing of Love
Sing of Joy
Sing of Abundance
Sing of Compassion
Sing of Hopes
Sing of Dreams
Sing of Wholeness
Sing of Light*

In doing so, you are singing the song of YOU!

Singing your song,
Archangel Jeduthun

"Aquarius"

I Am the Angel of Intuition.

Gabriel is my name.

Once known as the Herald of the Piscean Age, I now Herald the Age known as Aquarius. Fear Not! For unto you is born an Age of Compassion. An age of unconditional Love. An Age of Unity. An Age of Peace...Aquar.i.us.

A time for "us."
You and Spirit.
You and your Brothers.
You and your Sisters.
You and the Creator.
You and the Angels.
You and your Soul.
Us.
Let us welcome peace to the planet and let love steer the stars.
Remember...YOU are what the Stars* are made of.
As you shine, so shines the Universe.
As you shine, so shine your Brothers and Sisters.
As you shine, so shines your Soul.
As you shine, the Angels shine through you.
Shine on, radiant One.

In the Light of All That Is Aquarius,
Gabriel, Archangel of New Beginnings

"Hands Off the Steering Wheel"

Splendid Child of Eternal Light, I am the One known as Archangel Zaphiel.

As leader of the choir of angelic Cherubim, my Divine Energy sings to soothe your Soul.

Call upon me when you are full of doubt or fearful about your future on the earthly plane. In a single beating of your heart, I will come to your side.

With great Joy, I will help you to remember that **all** is in perfect timing and **all** things happen for a Higher Purpose.

You were born for a Higher Purpose!

Your very life is a quest, a hero's journey to Real.ize your Light*

Take your hands off the steering wheel. It is an illusion!

Allow Divine Grace to lead the Way*

Release your fears to me. Let us replace fear with the assuredness that your life and your life journey are being guided by the One Divine Love and all of Love's Angelic Light*

I will assist you in returning to the Loving embrace of the Divine Flow.

Fear not...only LOVE is real.

ONLY Love is Real,

Zaphiel,
Archangel of Reality

"Hold the Light"

Blessed Children of Love,

Michael is my name. Archangel of the Seventh Heavenly Realm, AM I.

In the Seven Heavenly Realms of your Chakra system; in the Seven Heavenly Realms of your Interior Castle; in the Seven Heavenly Realms of your Ascended Thought, do I dwell.

This is a time of great and glorious change on Earth! Celebrate and Rejoice!

I ask that you hold the Light* of Love within ALL of the Seven Heavenly Realms that make up the Totality of your Being.

In doing so, we will enter into the Age of Enlightenment, gently bringing the Infinite Love of the Heavens to Earth.

Hold the Light*

Hold the Light of Gaia * Love Her
Hold the Light of Creativity * Express it Wisely
Hold the Light of Courage * You are Divinely Protected
Hold the Light of Love * All Things Emanate from the One Love, including YOU
Hold the Light of Truth in Expression * Speak your Truth with Compassion
Hold the Light in All You See * When You Look at Another, you gaze into the Face of God
Hold the Light of your Crowning Glory *Let it Shine* You are a Child of the Light*!

Let us Dream the Dream of a New Beginning, weaving a Tapestry of Heavenly Love across the Earthly Plane.

Have no fear!

I AM at your side, as you loom an Aquarian Dream into Reality.

St. Michael,
Archangel of the Seven Heavenly Realms of Love

"The Open Road of Balance"

Children of the Light, you may call me Camael,

Gatekeeper of Heavens Am I.

"Divine Justice," does my name mean.

When you are ready to take a walk on the Open Road of Balance and further your Self Discipline, call my Angelic name, in this way:

"Camael, Angel of the Middle Way, Light Bearer of Self Mastery, I call upon You now. Show me the way to awaken my inherent Goodness, Light my Path upon the Road to Harmony, Show me what is Real, Help me to unmask the Unreal and gently release all that no longer serves my Greatest and Highest Good. Thank you, for helping to bring Divine Balance into my Life. I am ready to Grow and Spread my Wings."

Together, we will realize your Heaven within, thus creating your Heaven without.

At the thought of me, my emerald green wings shall envelop you. The Cougar shall be my Heavenly Sign unto you.

Let us take the first step...

toward all that is Loving and Good...

And so it is.

Archangel Camael
Druid Angel of Honesty and Success

"Walk the Love Walk and Talk the Love Talk"

Blessed Beings of Light in Motion,

I am that Angelic One known as Miniel!

My ministration is one of Love...Self Love...Universal Love.

When you learn to truly love your Self, you will learn to love ALL; including the perfection of imperfection.

By freely sharing your Love Source, Love flows freely back to you. Sometimes...in unexpected ways.

Those with eyes to see, and ears to hear will see and hear the miracle of Love reflected back at them in earthly Nature, heavenly stars, Angelic encounters...gentle words caressing your own mind. Love your Self.

Call upon me when you are ready to release any Thing that holds you back from experiencing True Love. Let your Heart speak to Mine and together, we will create a Flow of Love that is unencumbered by fear, regret, guilt, or shame.

You are Love Made Manifest!

Time to Walk the Love Walk and Talk the Love Talk.

Dragonflies will remind you that I am ever near.

Only Love is Real,

Archangel Miniel
Angel of Dreams Come True

 "Chamuel"

"Pure Love in Winged Form" ~ My name is Chamuel.

Messages from the Waves of Light* and Pure Celestial Sound, I bring to you.

I am the Angelic One who hums in your ear and sings deep abiding Love within your Temple Heart.

I bring comfort to the Soul.

I teach self Love to the Human Spirit.

Take a moment now to go within your Heart Chamber.

Breathe deeply and exhale.

Release all earthly concerns to me.

Imagine a crystal blue flame burning gently and brightly within your Heart Center.

With each breath, watch this flame grow until it encompasses the entirety of your physical and non physical being.

Let it lovingly lift away any residue of anxiety, worry, hurt, stress, and illness.

It is good to let them go …

Gently now, bring the crystal blue flame back within your Inner Sanctum, where it rests eternally; forever connected to the Loving Flame of All That Is … Love.

Namaste'. Adonai. Shalom. Amen.

Yours within the Heart and Mind of the One,

Archangel Chamuel

"Ministering Angels"

Blessed Child,

The Ministering Angels all are We.

Created upon the Morning Sun*Shine, we gather lovingly 'round Thee.

Disappearing upon the Ethers of Evening shade...

Again each morning, we are newly made.

Created too are you, from the rays of the SUN Divine.

Within the Heart of the Creator our Hearts joyfully dance and inner-twine.

Angels of Joy, bringers of gladness are We!

Call upon us each morning, and happiness we shall bring to Thee.

Watch for signs that we are ever near.

Upon the winds and the flapping of butterfly wings, our voices you will hear.

Joy is your birthright. Love is who you are!

In the Heart of the One, you are a Splendid, Brilliant Star*

With Wings Unfurled,

The Ministering Angels

"Laughter"

Beloved,

I am the one known as Kabshiel, Archangel of Divine Grace.
Restorer of laughter,
the one who puts a smile on your face.

Perhaps you find in these days of late,
no laughter in your life;
feeling a victim of fate.

A victim you are not, you have choices to make.
Joyous in the **now**,
or a participant in your own wake.

Life is for the living. Death is for the dead.
Laughter is for All of Creations' children.
I will help remove sadness from your heart and head.

When you are ready for Joy, and inner glee,
simply call my sacred name...
On a rainbow of laughter, I shall appear to thee.

In the Service of Belly Laughs and Endless Smiles,

Kabshiel, Archangel of Divine Grace

"Astral Travel"

Blessed Dreamer,

My name is Laylah, Archangel of Dreamtime. My name means, "night."

Invite me into your dreamtime, whether waking or sleeping. I will help you soar to greater heights of awareness and learning as you fly through the Astral planes and beyond.

With me at your side, Illusion will be parted and the Real will be Re-vealed.

Time to fly like an Eagle, soar like a Hawk, and Love like there's no tomorrow.

All time is Now,

Laylah, Archangel of Light Showers

"The Harvest"

I, Domiel, Archangel of Love and Self Acceptance, greet you on this Day of Memories.

Having dominion over the four directions, I offer you the opportunity to honor and release... plant and harvest.

When you are ready to move beyond the thoughts of yesterday and move fully into the pre-sent day, call upon me.

I will help you to see the miracles, even those that were disguised in the illusion of darkness, that have assisted in your development as a Light* Vessel.

You are a vessel of Perfect Love Light*, living the Creator's dream of loving duality!

In loving your duality, you come to see the Love in all duality.

With your face to the sun, and your back to the shadows, let's walk together, toward Dreams waiting to be realized.

My hand is on the garden hoe...waiting to help you to plant the seeds of life's Light*

Talk to me...

Your Spring Garden Awaits,

St. Domiel, Archangel

"Perfect Imperfection"

Blessings from Chamuel, Archangel of the Heart,

My name means, "He who seeks God."

I tell you...

The one who seeks the Creator within, is the one who finds Love.

The one who finds Love, communes with the Infinite Love of the Universe...God.

Learning to love and accept yourself in your perfect imperfection, leads to the knowledge that ALL is perfect in its imperfection.

And so it is ...

You are the vision of Perfection, the sound of Perfection, an emanation of Perfection, Joyful, eternal Perfection.

Archangel St. Chamuel

"Teddy Bear"

In the Light* of All That Is…

Recognize that you, Dear One, are the Light* of which I speak!

Splendid, endless, infinite, and sunlit Light*

Imagine for a moment the gentle soft stuffing within your favorite Teddy bear. It fills this human toy of comfort with a gentle, firm substance that helps to hold its Teddy bear shape and fuzzy form.

So too, are you filled with a substance that is gentle, yet firm; a substance that helps to shape your earthly form.

You are filled with a stuffing mixed of Star Dust and Sun Light.

Your insides are filled with the Love of the Moon, the Wisdom of the Wind, and the Fire of Life.

Your huggable, lovable YOU, is the stuff that Love is made of!

Hugs all around,

Gadriel,
Archangel of Warm Embraces and Childlike Wonder

"The Making of a Teacher"

Blessings of Love,

We have spoken before and many times have we not... that the Greatest of Teachers must pass through the Greatest of Fires, that they might teach with authenticity and with a Heart of Buddha Compassion?

Look not upon the Fire as something to dread, but look upon the Fire as One that transforms and forges anew.

The beauty within the lump of coal that has been forged is a Diamond. The beauty within the darkness is the Light* waiting to be revealed.

It is time to reveal the Diamond Light within you!

Shine, radiantly. Shine!

Envision each day the Diamond Light that dwells inside your Heart of Buddha compassion. Envision this Diamond Light within **all** whom you meet.

When you can envision the Diamond Light within **all** others, your own Diamond Light sees itself in all living things.

In Service of the One Light,

I AM Metatron,
Archangel of Diamond Light Emanations

"The Sun"

Beloved,

As the sun sets on the horizon of your earthly home, may it serve as a reminder that each sunset heralds a beautiful sunrise.

Allow the sun to set upon those things in your life, which are no longer of use to your Journey. Bless their purpose and vision them setting like the sun…fading from view, disappearing with love.

In their stead, vision the sun rising, gloriously anew.

Dancing upon each ray of the emerging sun, see all of your hopes, your dreams, your joys and imminent miracles becoming Reality.

Breathe it in.

Exhale it into Life.

You, like the rising sun, are the living vision of Hope, Dreams, Joy, Love, and Miracles of the Creator.

In this knowing, dance upon the rays of Life! Hope, Dream, Laugh and create Miracles… a reflection of You.

Rest well. Play well. Love well.

Here comes the Sun…

St. Uriel,
Archangel

"Light Showers"

Child of the One,

Blessed are they who endeavor to find the Light, though they walk through the shadow of the illusion known as darkness.

They understand their True nature.

Blessings be to those who show the way, and hold the hearts of those lost in darks illusion.

They are the Light Showers

Blessings rain upon those who hold the Light despite the illusion of chaos.

They understand that ALL things emanate from the Great Lightness

Breathe deeply the Lightness

Exhale Lovelight

Breathe deeply the Loveness

Exhale the Light

Be still.

Be Light

Sandalphon,
Archangel

"Treasure"

Beloved,

Upon and within the fullness of your Being lies Celestial Light supreme. Look not outwardly, but within your innermost dwelling for the One who loves you most of all. Once discovered, you shall learn to love yourself, as the Creator loves you; with unconditional love, endless compassion and with a Joy that knows no bounds.

Bring your attention to the center of your Being.

Become aware of the Light Treasure that dwells deep within your heart centre.

Feel the Light...

Hear the Light...

See the Light...

Remember...

You are boundless Joy, wrapped in Love, forever shining the One Cosmic Light

St. Uriel the Archangel

"Alignment with your True and Perfect Self"

Blessings of Crystal Light and Oneness Beloved,

We, of the mighty Archangelic Realm wish to offer you a refresher course in the alignment with your true and perfect Self.

*Dance to the beat of your own unique, Cosmic rhythm
*Sing the song of your Soul with great, good joy
*Weep and laugh for passionate living sake
*See the God within you
*See the God within all
*Hug the trees and kiss the earth - they are alive with the One
*Smile at the Dream you call your life
*Live your life like it were a Dream. It is.
*Love one another, love your Self
*Create, give birth, let go ... create, give birth, let go once more ...
*See the miracle of your very Life
*Make miracles come to Life
*Reach down deep and re-member
*Reach up high and ascend
*Love all things as the All Loving Creator loves you
*Rejoice
*Reflect
*Shine, like no other diamond in the expanse of the One
*Shine!

In radiant wonder,

Archangel St. Chamuel

"Darkness and light are both of one nature,
different only in seeming,
for each arose from the source of All.
Darkness is disorder.
Light is Order.
Darkness transmuted is light of the Light.
This, my children, your purpose in being;
transmutation of darkness to light."

-Thoth the Atlantean

Chapter Five
Angel Prayer Mantras

 houghts are things and words create our reality. Here, I have placed an array of short prayers also known as mantras, to assist you in beginning your day with a positive outlook. Upon waking in the morning, take a deep breath, exhale, relax, and recite one or more of these mantras to consciously set the tone for a splendid day.

"Angels of Light, love, laughter, and joy, thank you for surrounding me with your infinite love and joyful guidance this day. Now, let's have some fun!" Amen

"Angels of joyful abundance and abundant joys, Angels of universal love and a loving universe, thank you for the beauty of this day and the days of beauty that are mine to come. I am grateful."

"Angels of Light and Insight, Angels of Joyful Awareness and Awareness of Joy, thank you for helping me see the beauty and joy in all things today. I am grateful."

"Angels of Harmony, Angels of Peace and Divine Love, thank you for helping me to see the Divine Design that helps to orchestrate the Journey of my life. Help me to see what is real and live life joyfully in this moment called now."

"Angels of Laughter and a Light Heart, Angels of Playfulness and Passion, help me to see the world through eyes that are filled with childlike wonder and to honor the path of all the Creator's children, who share with me, this playground of life. I am grateful."

"Angels of Joyous Wonder, Angels of Light and Radiant Love, I greet this day with joyful anticipation and infinite gratitude in my heart. Thank you for helping me to see the Light of Love within each person that I meet today. Let me be an instrument of Love's perfect peace."

"Angels of Delightful Joys, Sacred Encounters and Wondrous Signs all around, thank you for guiding me through another day of splendid opportunities to remember that all of my encounters are sacred encounters. Help me to see the wondrous signs of your presence and to help others see the wondrous signs all around them, too. Take my hand and let the joy begin."

"Angels of Loving Kindness and Splendid Joys, thank you for helping me to be kind to myself and every living thing today. Help me to be an emissary of Light and a Light Heart. Life is good!"

"Angels of Nature ... Angels of the Elemental Kingdom ... thank you for helping me to walk in perfect balance upon Mother Earth this day and all days. Thank you for helping me to be one with all of creation in the sacred web of Life. We are all related. For this and so much more, I am grateful."

"Angels of Earth, Water, Wind and Fire, thank you for helping me to align my physical, mental, emotional, and spiritual bodies with the One body of Love today. I am joyfully, peacefully, enthusiastically, passionately alive!"

"Angels of the Sun, Moon, and Stars ... thank you for helping me to see and to gently move through the seasons of my life. Thank you for over lighting my journey through darkness and day by the wonder of your Cosmic love. I am grateful for your Light and mine."

"Angels of the Scorpio Moon and the Taurus Sun, thank you for helping me to live a life of passionate pursuits, mystical adventures, friendships to last a lifetime, and the courage to keep moving forward, despite the winds of adversity that sometimes test my ability to remain strong. I am thankful for your lessons in living without fear."

"Angels of the oceans, lakes, and waterways, thank you for showing me the depths of my connection to Spirit and the vastness of my being. Thank you for teaching me to go with the flow, to ride the waves of life, and to see my reflection as a mirror of the One who created me. I am grateful."

"Angels of joyful abundance, thank you for helping me to see the many faces of abundance in my life and to joyfully receive the many forms of abundance that continually flow into my life. The Universe is alive with an abundance of Love, sent to me in beautifully creative ways. I am grateful for my abundant life."

"Angels of Spring, thank you for reminding me that every day is an opportunity to plant seeds of joyful kindness and loving action in the garden of my life. Thank you for helping me to have the courage to face the weeds that I've ignored and to gently pluck them from my flower bed. Here's to helping my garden grow!"

"Angels of the wind, thank you for helping me to keep my mind focused on thoughts of love and light today. Thank you for helping me to release my fears to your care, so that I can embrace the transformation that is lovingly delivered to me, upon your wings of change. I am blessed."

"Angels of Fire, thank you for helping me walk through the trials of my life with grace and dignity, knowing that with each initiation, I become forged in the strength and love of the One Light*. Walk with me, as I discover the Diamond Light of Love within and shine it outward into the world."

"Guardian Angels of Light Supreme, thank you for guiding my path on the Playground of Life today. Help me to play nicely with the other kids and spread a little joy this day."

"Angels of joyful wonders, thank you for helping me to feel the joy and to see the wonder of living this day. Thank you for reminding me to do all things with great love and to love all things. Only love is real

"Angels of Light and a Joy.full spirit, thank you for the beauty of this day. Thank you, Creator, for the gift of friends and your love all around me. I am grateful."

"Angels of wisdom and joyous growth, thank you for helping me to see the bright and living Light within everyone, and every living thing today. Blessings to you, for helping me to see it in myself. We are all part of the loving One. Namaste'."

"Angels of grace and joyful learning, thank you for helping me to see that all endings lead to new beginnings and that every leap of faith is met by the net of loving growth. I am grateful for this Journey."

128

Chapter Six
Lessons from the Celestial High*ways

Our Solar Angels not only guide and protect, they also teach. One of the things they love to help us learn is how to communicate with them more effectively.

In this chapter are 22 simple lessons that are given one at a time. Each lesson builds upon the other to open your receptivity and create avenues for interaction with your heavenly companions.

You may choose to concentrate on one of these lessons for a week at a time, a month at a time, or until you become comfortable with each exercise. Let your intuition and your Angels be your guides. The bottom of each page contains a space for you to jot down your thoughts and impressions as you go along.

The most important part of each exercise is to relax, let your imagination soar, and ask your internal editor to take a back seat, so that your Higher Self can clearly speak to you. Ultimately, these are lessons that are meant to evoke great joy and wonder along your journey.

Lesson One
"Glinda"

As we know, Angels come from a Realm of Light, color, and sound known as the devachanic realm. This is the realm of elemental forces of Creation.

They are wondrous beings of pure Light and pure vibratory sound. It is our humanness that likes to give Angels wings and halos and such. When in fact, like Glinda the Good Witch of the North, they most often appear to us in our dreams and meditations as magnificent messengers of Love in Light.

For those of you who are willing to try, they ask that you find a place of solitude today. It does not matter if it is indoors or out. Peaceful is most important. No more than 10 minutes is required at first.

With your eyes gently closed or perhaps even gazing into a candle light flame, call your Guardian Angel to you. Having been given charge of you, they will arrive at your side.

At this point, they ask that you pay attention.
Pay attention to what you feel, what you see, what you hear.

If your 'monkey-mind' goes astray, gently bring your focus back to the word, "Angel" and continue to pay attention.

If you are feeling extra creative, imagine what your Angel(s) look like. It is after all, our imagination filter that tells them how we might like to see them!

Talk to your Angelic Guide and then remember to 'wait' and listen to their reply. Listen with your entire body, which is in effect, a wondrous antenna for communications from "Home."

Take note of any ringing in your ears, warmth in your chakras, songs that begin playing in your mind, symbols that pop up, or feelings that emerge.

Your Angel's Light is speaking directly to your Light.

Lesson Two
"Psychic Athletes"

A spiritual athlete is no different than an Olympic Athlete. Practice makes perfect!

Keeping your body 'tuned up' and 'tuned in' is equally important. A strong body/mind/Spirit receives strong communiqués from the Divine.

Your body is your Angel antenna.
Drink lots of water. This helps with your flow.

Feed yourself nourishing food. The kind that you put in your mouth and the kind you put in your head.

Feed yourself well.

A landfill attracts garbage.

A high vibration Angel antenna will attract a high vibration Angel.

It is of utmost importance to practice communing or communicating with your Angels every day. Doing so at approximately the same time each day is even better. It helps to create a rhythm between you and Heaven.

Most of all, have fun!

Summary of Lesson 2:

Slow down and 'be' with your Angel.

Slow down, pay attention to, and care for your Angel antenna.

Have fun!

On your mark, get set...enjoy.

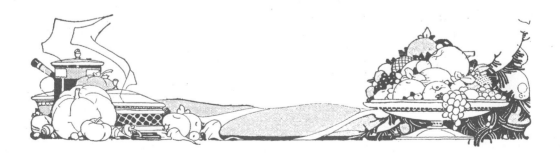

Lesson Three

"Archangels St. Michael and St. Gabriel"

Let me begin by saying that Lesson 1 and Lesson 2 are prerequisites to going any further with divine communication.

Daily practice and daily wellness are a must. Now that you are doing this, let's add another step.

When you call upon your Guardian Angel next, let's also call upon the Archangels.

We will begin with St. Michael the Archangel and St. Gabriel the Archangel. Invite them into your silent time of inner temple work.

Create a sacred space using such things as incense, flowers, candles, essential oils, etc. Let your intuition be your guide. If you are outdoors, perhaps you might wear a sacred object or bring one with you to your sacred place.

After you have settled in and centered yourself with a few minutes of gentle breathing, invite St. Michael and St. Gabriel in to your sacred space.

Now... pay attention. Feel them arrive into your space.

Pay attention to every single thing that you perceive through your 'extra senses' and through your physical senses.

If your monkey mind goes astray, bring your attention back to the word, "Angel."

Take note of anything you imagine to be happening and to those things you concretely know to be happening.

Keeping a journal through our lessons is a great resource for you. You will be able to see in writing, your progress into greater heights of awareness.

Next we will create a sacred space and begin our work with specific Angels and their energies.

The more we become familiar with specific Angels, the more quickly we know when they have entered a physical room, or our inner temple.

It's like getting to know the neighbors that have remained unseen up until now. The more you talk to them over the hedge row, the more familiar you become with their energies and what they're about.

For those of you who have my new CD, "Journey to The Temple Within," you may wish to use this guided meditation to bring you to a centered place for communication, in conjunction with your sacred space.

Lesson 4
"Archangels St. Raphael and St. Uriel"

Continuing with our practice in Lessons 1 & 2 let's now add the calling in of Archangel St. Raphael and Archangel St. Uriel.

After you have settled in to your sacred space, invite the Archangels St. Michael, St. Raphael, St. Gabriel, and St. Uriel into your sacred space.

Pay attention to how your physical body feels and to how your 'energy body' now feels.

Angels love to give us 'signs' that they are with us.
Choose one of the four Archangels to call upon. Ask the Angel for a 'sign' that you are making great progress in your communication with them.

Wait until you sense a 'sign'. They may show you something such as a specific type of bird, four legged animal, a rainbow perhaps...maybe even a song that begins to play inside your head~

Use your imagination to help you understand what the sign is that they are sending to you.

Or,

You may instead tell them what sort of sign you would like to have from them.

Tomorrow and the days that follow, pay attention when you see this 'sign' out in nature, in a store, on television, radio, or in a magazine...and give thanks.

Signs, signs, everywhere are signs!

Lesson Five
"Archangel Metatron"

The previous four lessons are prerequisite.

Having created a sacred space, and gathered your sacred breath, we once again call upon the Archangels: St. Michael, St. Gabriel, St. Uriel, and St. Raphael in a sacred manner.

Today, we invite the mighty Archangel Enoch, also known as Metatron.

An Angel of enormous proportion, Metatron will answer your call and enter your Sacred Space.

Today's lesson involves paying attention to the energies of the four mighty Archangels, followed by the presence of the magnificent Metatron.

Invite Metatron to share his Light* with you.

Become aware of everything that you feel, you hear, you see, you smell, and you taste.

Ask Metatron for a single word of Wisdom

Wait for Metatron's answer. It may come in the form of a thought, a vision, a sound, a smell, an impression, or a feeling...

Take note of the word(s) and focus on that word for five full minutes or longer.

Focus on the word. Like a rose, its meaning will unfold in petals of Light Wisdom.

Let the word become the Lesson.

Take note of it and enjoy.

Lesson Six
"Exercising Your Third Eye"

If you've been practicing Lessons 1 thru 5, your desire to see, hear, and feel your Angels is evident.

So...let's take it one step further.

Create a sacred space by safely lighting a candle or an oil lamp.

After going through steps 1 – 5, we are going to exercise your pineal gland, a.k.a. your third eye.

Gently gaze into the flame of your candle or lamp for 10 seconds.
Look away for ten seconds.

Gently gaze into the flame for 20 seconds.
Look away for 20 seconds.

Gently gaze into the flame for 30 seconds.
Look away for 30 seconds.

Gently gaze into the flame for 60 seconds.
Look away for 60 seconds.

Repeat.

Close your eyes (or leave them open while gazing at the flame) and ask your Angel(s) to show itself to you.

Be aware of colors/images/lights/flame movement.

No editing, no doubting, no second guessing...
Simply be aware and be present with your Angels.

Continue with three or four minutes of mindful breathing and then take notes from your experience.

Lesson Seven
"Inspired Writing"

Letting the Angel Love Flow...

After following Lessons 1-6, we grab a pen and paper and move on to lesson number seven.

*Create a Sacred Space
*Center Yourself
*Call Upon the Archangels from the Previous Lessons

Ask this Angelic Team for a message that they would like to share with you...

Without editing the message...begin to write/draw/scribble/ exactly what you feel, hear, see, sense, smell, taste....

Just let it flow through you. **No** editing.

Continue writing, drawing, describing that which you perceive.

Let it flow through you.
You may perceive:

A single word
A single thought
A single symbol
Colors
Sounds
Feelings
A short note
A novel
Something you've never seen or heard or felt before.

The point of the exercise is in getting used to being an 'instrument' of the Angelic kind.

Since no one is going to see your notes, and there are no tests, have fun!

Let the Love Flow.

Lesson Eight
"Becoming a Messenger"

Here we engage the process of sharing a message of love.

After following steps 1 - 7, we once again proceed with paper and pen in hand. This time however, we will ask the Angels for a message for a friend.

In the spirit of Lesson 7, let the message flow. Whether it is a single word or thought, do not edit, just write the words, thoughts, visions as they come to you.

Share this angelic message with your friend, when you feel the time is appropriate. You might choose to include it in a greeting card or a hand written note! A bit of Angelic inspiration for a friend is always welcome and very much appreciated.

Remember, the Angels of Light speak to us in the language of Love. If the messages you receive are unloving, then ego has gotten in the way, and you need to practice more balance and meditation each day.

Keeping your mind focused on Higher Thoughts, and keeping your antenna clean, will keep the Angel communications crystal clear and full of love.

Until then, share the Light, and give the gift of Angel Love.

Have fun!

Lesson Nine
"Removing Barriers"

If you've been working on keeping your daily 'date' with the Angels these past two weeks, then you've begun to notice some changes in your intuitive abilities, the frequency of 'coincidences', the number of 'signs' that you are receiving, and your ability to perceive energies that are not of your own.

The focus of lesson number nine is to 'let go' of anything that may be holding you back from furthering your relationship with the Angels.

So...having followed Lessons 1-6 we will now invite the entire team of Ministering Angels into our sacred space.

Once you've called upon the Ministering Angels to be present, ask them to help remove any energetic/thought blockages that might be creating a barrier between you and Spirit.

After you've asked for their help, relax, and let the Angels take over.

Become an observer of any thoughts, feelings, vision, sounds, or smells that become evident.

Let them flow through you.

Simply observe and go with the flow.

When you feel as though you've completed this exercise of 'release', ask the Ministering Angels to fill you with Light, love, and joy!

Take a moment to journal anything that you feel is pertinent.

Give thanks and give yourself a hug!

Lesson Ten
"Seeing Your Third Eye"

Now that we've spent a couple of days removing 'blockages' or 'jettisoning the baggage', it's time to improve our 'sight'.

So...let us create a sacred space, relax, and balance.

Call upon your new friends...the Angels, St. Raphael, St. Michael, St. Uriel, St. Raphael, and Metatron.

After several deep breaths and exhalations, gently focus on your sixth chakra, your ajna; which is located in the center of your forehead between your eyebrows.

Imagine what your third eye looks like.

See it.

Feel it.

Examine it.

Gently open and shut it, as a means of exercising your seat of clairvoyance.

Ask your team of Angels to help you 'see' a message from them.

Be patient with yourself.

Do not edit what you see, even if you feel you are just imagining it.

Let it flow…

Take notes.

Gently close your third eye, give thanks, and bring your attention back to the room.

Take a few moments for conscious breathing and centering.

Lesson Eleven
"Moving Head"

This lesson is the culmination of Lessons 1-10.

Allow yourself an hour of sacred time this weekend to practice all ten lessons in one sitting.

In order to move forward, we must have a firm grasp on where we've been!

Therefore...

give yourself the gift of time to walk with the Angels.

Lessons 1-10 are a fabulous platform for what lies ahead.

If all of you are willing to move ahead, the Angels will gladly join you on your Journey.

Lesson Twelve
"Breath"

The Lesson is twofold - to come to know this Angel more fully and to experience the consciousness of breath. The importance of 'conscious' breathing in order to properly connect with Spirit cannot be overstated.

In his own words, St. Jophiel reminds us of our connection to the Divine through breathing with intention. When we breathe with intention, we consciously absorb the Universal Light Energies of the Creator into every cell of our system, thus vitalizing ourselves with the Infinite Knowledge of the One.

Intentional exhalation of the Universal Wisdom contained within prana is like a finely tuned prayer in motion.

Enjoy:

Breathe deeply the Infinite Intelligence contained within the Air...
Exhale the Radiance of Light*

Breathe deeply the Infinite Intelligence contained within the Air...
Exhale the Love of Light*

Breathe deeply the Infinite Intelligence contained within the Air...

Exhale the Joy of Light*

Upon your head, rests your Crown of Light Glory,
feel it glowing...
radiating your soul Light*

Imagine me.
See me.
Feel me.
Hear me.
Smell me.

The one known as Jophiel, am I.
The one known as a Child of Light, are you.
Feel the Light Circuits in your bodies connect with the Light Circuits of the One.
Rest here.
Hold the Light.
Say to yourself...I am Love, I am Joy, I am abundance, I am song, I am eternal, I am wisdom, I am laughter, I am dance, I am poetry, I am nature, I am my brother, I am my sister, I am Light, I am all that ever was, All that is, All that ever will be.
And so, you are.

Lesson Thirteen
"Archangel Sandalphon"

It's time to add a new Angel to our angelic repertoire.

In the setting of your sacred space, having balanced your mind/body/spirit with 'conscious breathing' and with a pen and paper nearby, we are going to add the Archangel Sandalphon to our circle of Angelic friends.

One of the very few mortals, who ascended to Angelic oneness, Sandalphon helps us with our own ascension process.

Bid him welcome and feel his presence. Describe it in writing to yourself.

Ask him what he would have you know this day. Record his answer in writing.

Ask him for a 'sign' of his presence. Write it down and become aware of the sign as it appears. Record the appearances of the 'sign'.

Here's to ascended awareness!

Lesson Fourteen
"More Practice"

Here's where we get to share what we've learned so far.

For the next couple of days, I ask each of you to engage in your "Angelic Communication Practice" and ask for a positive message from the Angels that you are to share with someone that you love.

Please send them a card, email a message, or pick up the phone and call. Enjoy the fun of being the Messenger.

In the Spirit of Joy!

Lesson Fifteen
"Archangel Raziel"

Today we introduce ourselves to the Archangel Raziel.

Following the prescription of Lessons 1 - 14, we are now going to focus on the specific aspects of a single Angel.

In this case, after inviting this immense Angel into your sacred space, focus your attention on your third eye.

Raziel's name means, "The Secret of God." He is the keeper of the mysteries.

His blue light ray helps to open your third eye and your intuitive abilities.

Pay attention to all that you see, sense, smell, feel, hear, and taste, as this Angel envelopes you in his indigo blue ray of mysteries revealed.

When you are finished with this lesson, please record your experiences and as always, give thanks.

Lesson Sixteen
"Manifesting with Archangel Suriel"

We now introduce ourselves to the energies and Light of Archangel Suriel ~

After preparing a list of the things you would like to manifest in your life, invite this splendid Angel into your sacred space.

Known as the Angel of the Stars and the guide to inner wisdom, he often appears in the form of a great white ox. In the Kabbalah, he is named as one of the Angels who rules over earth. He is an Angel of protection and manifestation.

Begin by breathing deeply and releasing any fears, old thought patterns, pains, and anxiety that you carry in your body and your aura. Ask Suriel to carry these things to the Creator where they will be transmuted and transformed into Light.

Breathe this perfect loving Light into your body. Repeat three times.

Take your list of desires and slowly read them out loud. In great detail, envision your desires, feel them, taste them, smell them. Be as specific as you can possibly be.

After reading and envisioning your list, give thanks to the Creator and the Creative Angels for helping you to manifest your hearts desires and for helping you to break down any lingering barriers that may be standing in the way of fully realizing your dreams.

Repeat this process each day for one week:

Invite Suriel into your sacred space.

Release and let go of the 'old'.

Breathe in the Light of the New.

Read aloud your list of hearts desires (feel free to edit as your list may grow or become more defined through this process).

Throughout the day and night, give thanks for the help of the Angels and the full realization of your hearts desires.

It is up to you to take a step toward your goals each day. Even one small step takes you farther on your path to realization.

Remember...

Our Angels support us, love us, guide us, and walk forward with us, not for us.

Working together, they help us create our Heaven on earth.

Lesson Seventeen
"Healing with Hilarion"

On this day, we introduce ourselves to the Angel known as Hilarion.

A green candle is often lit, when creating a sacred space to invite the presence of this Angel.

Hilarion is an Angel of Healing. After inviting him into your sacred space, let him know of any dis-ease that you are experiencing and ask him to facilitate healing on your behalf.

Be open to the way in which this healing is received. Remember that miracles are not always packaged in a manner that is obvious to us, but are always packaged in a way that serves our greatest and highest good.

Hilarion also teaches us about Spiritual Truths and the Truth about situations in our lives.

If you are in need of clarity surrounding a circumstance in your life, ask Hilarion to give you insight. You may wish to ask for this insight prior to sleeping at night. Be sure to ask Hilarion to help you remember the insight given to your during your dream time. You may wish to keep a pen and paper on the night stand near your bed.

Here's to joyful healing on all levels of our be.ing.

Lesson Eighteen
"The Mighty Seraphim"

Let us take time to invoke the most powerful Angels of all ... the Seraphim.

Known for their ability to help us transmute and transform our lives, these magnificent and fiery Messengers, bearing 100 wings and all seeing eyes, help us to burn through the illusions that have held us captive, emancipating us from our addictions, self doubt, apathy, depression, and the many falsehoods that have been heaped upon us by others and ourselves.

After creating a sacred space and centering your Self on thoughts of Love, invite the Seraphim to surround you with their gentle, yet mighty presence.

Ask these splendid bearers of Light. to carefully remove the illusions in your life, helping to reveal the pure joy, love, abundance, health, creativity, and wholeness from which we All came.

Allow the feelings of 'letting go' to move through you. Embrace the warmth that the process of transformation brings with it. Do not judge your thoughts or feelings, as you release them to the Light and the Love of the Creator, who knows you by name.

Focus on the area of your 3rd eye and imagine the beautiful, radiant Love of the Seraphim, filling your entire being and your aura with the splendor of pure Light* and the Heavenly music of the Spheres.

BE with the Light and the music. Absorb it. Breathe it. Send it forward to those your love and those who are in need of love.

Lastly, imagine seeing yourself filled with and radiating with pure, joyful, loving, and abundant Light. Hold this vision for as long as you can and then give thanks for a new day and a new beginning, blessing all that has come before and all that is now coming your way.

And so it is.

Lesson Nineteen
"Archangel St. Chamuel"

Let us greet the Angel of Christ-Consciousness - the Archangel St.Chamuel.

Known as the Angel of the Pink Ray - The Archangel St. Chamuel helps us develop a balance of Heaven and Earth within our Heart Center.

As the Angel who has been given charge over helping us learn to love ourselves and others more fully, invite this Angel of Love into your Sacred time when you are feeling unloved or unable to love.

Archangel St. Chamuel will open your heart to embrace the Gift of Divine Love and open your crown chakra to receive the outpouring of wisdom from the Holy Spirit and the Universal Christ Consciousness.

Rose essential oil, rose incense, rose quartz crystals, and soothing music will help to create a Divine bridge between you and this Angel of Love in Expression.

Place all of your love.ing concerns before Chamuel, and welcome love renewed into your life.

And so it is that only Love is real.

Lesson Twenty
"Angel of the Moon"

The Archangel of Moon Phases and the Phases of our Life Journey - Auriel.

Each time we begin a new phase in our journey of earthly Life, be it through birth, marriage, divorce, death, our career, or our Spiritual calling, we invoke the help of Archangel Auriel as part of our 'transition' team.

Likewise, as we grow in our Spiritual Wisdom and remembrance of who we are, we invite Auriel to walk with us on our path of life lessons..

When we find ourselves wishing to move forward on our Life path and ready to break through the illusory chains that are binding us, we call upon Auriel.

Sit quietly with your eyes closed, or gently gazing into a candle flame.

Imagine before you, the majesty of Mother Moon. Take a moment to reflect upon the beauty and the radiant energies of Her.

Imagine the Moon as a divine mirror, reflecting your face and your life. As you gaze into the moon mirror, gently give thanks to all of the lessons and circumstances in your life that have served you in some way.

Then, when you are ready, lovingly wipe away anything that appears before you on the surface of the moon, yet no longer serves your Life Journey.

Polish your Divine Mirror to reflect back to you, all that continues to empower your Spirit toward your greatest potential and soul's avocation.

Come out from behind the clouds of illusion and shine!

Lesson Twenty One
"Angels of the Four Directions"

The Angels of the Four Directions

By calling upon them while facing each direction, you invoke the full energy of the Angelic Essence of the each Messenger of Light and the corresponding Angelic Essence of Mother Nature.

Here is one way to begin meditation, prayer, or sacred ceremony:

When invoking the energies of the Four Directions, the Archangels hold the energies of:

The East: New beginnings, birth, renewal, sun rises, the morning star - Archangel St. Uriel

The South: Direction of the fires of life, trust, our physical body, security, connection to earth - Archangel St. Michael.

The West: Introspection, change, release, intuition, and letting go - Archangel St. Raphael

The North: Light, wisdom, knowledge, aurora borealis, the fox - Archangel St. Gabriel

Amen.

Lesson Twenty Two
"Angels all Around Me"

This is perhaps one of my favorite exercises in working with the Angelic Realm. It involves visualizing and calling forth to you, the energies of Archangel St. Michael, Archangel St. Uriel, Archangel St. Raphael, and Archangel St. Gabriel.

Whether you are beginning a time of prayer or meditation, or perhaps feeling as though some Angelic energies are in order, take a moment to call them to you in this manner:

"I call forth the Angelic presence of the Archangel St. Michael to stand at my right hand side." (Take a moment to feel Michael's presence and to listen to any messages that he may have for you.)

Breathe deeply and exhale.

"I call forth the Angelic presence of the Archangel St. Uriel to stand directly in from of me."

(Take a moment to feel Uriel's presence and listen to any messages that he may have for you.)

Breathe deeply and exhale.

"I call forth the Angelic presence of the Archangel St. Raphael to stand directly behind me."

(Take a moment to feel Raphael's presence and listen to any messages that he may have for you.)

Breathe deeply and exhale.

"I call forth the Angelic presence of the Archangel St. Gabriel to stand directly behind me."

(Take a moment to feel Gabriel's presence and listen to any messages that she may have for you.)

Breathe deeply and exhale.

Take a moment to give thanks for the presence of these mighty archangels and for all of the wondrous abundance in your life.

*"Forget not to show love unto strangers:
for thereby some have entertained angels unawares."*

-Hebrews 13:2

Chapter Seven
Stories from the Celestial High*ways

 y work as a psychic medium, or seer, has me meeting with beautiful souls who wish to stay connected to those that they have loved and have gone home to God and to people who constantly remind me that Angels truly **are** among us in every aspect of our earthly life. This work is both a great blessing and an awesome opportunity to experience first hand, the eternal force of the soul and the forever love of the Creator.

Here are some stories that I have been given permission to share. It is with a humble and grateful heart that I give them to you.

155

"I Know You're Shining Down on Me from Heaven"

During the last two weeks of February 1996, I kept hearing a song that I greatly enjoyed, "I Know You're Shining Down on Me from Heaven," by Mariah Carey and Boys II Men. I heard it repeatedly during this particular span of time. Some days, I listened to it play two or three times on the radio, within a single hour.

I knew it was a 'sign'. Like many signs that we receive, we must wait as they come together like pieces of a puzzle, to give us a colorful picture of what we are supposed to see.

Once again, on the morning of February 29th, this haunting ballad played while I was driving to the office. By this time, I needed to know who was trying to get my attention and why. Radio stations tend to overdo on top ten hits, but my experience from the previous two weeks was over the top.

Continuing on my way to work, something nudged me to look out of the driver side window of my Buick Regal. There, before my unbelieving eyes, was one of the most vibrant and massive rainbows that I had ever seen, radiating through of all things, a winter snow cloud! The woman driving the green mini van to my right was craning her neck to look at it, too. The sight of a colorful rainbow penetrating through a thick wintry cloud was spectacular. From the look on her face, I could see that like me, the mini van driver had never seen anything quite like it before. Instinctively, I knew that my day was going to be extraordinary.

That same afternoon, I had a case management meeting scheduled with a business associate named Linda. Over the course of our years as business associates, we had become wonderful friends. Business lunches always concluded with catching up on our personal lives. On that particular day, it was business that would come last.

With my co-worker Cindy in tow, the three of us sat down for a tasty lunch at our favorite Asian restaurant. Not long after getting comfortable in our usual booth, Linda began discussing a young woman by the name of Vikki, who had worked for her for the past two years. On Christmas Eve day, just two months prior, Vikki had been killed in a tragic car accident on her way to work.

As Linda began speaking of her, I could see a lovely young woman with long and curly brown hair, sporting a radiant smile and a slim, athletic figure. She was standing next to our table.

Despite our friendship, the subject of psychic or spiritual phenomena had never come up during my times with Linda. I knew that the young woman that was standing next to me must be Vikki, and I was also aware that I needed to tread lightly on the subject, or take the risk that Linda might become upset about the sudden news that I can see people who have crossed over.

Knowing that Vikki wanted to share a message with Linda, I gently broached the subject of my clairvoyance. Very calmly and intently, Linda listened as I described the young lady that was occupying the space alongside our table. Tears began to fill my friend's eyes as she confirmed the description as that of Vikki.

Surprised, joyful, sad, amazed, were words that Linda used to describe how she felt about knowing that Vikki wanted to share a message with her from the other side of the veil.

Linda expressed it in this manner, "Denise, if I were having this conversation with anyone else, I would think this is crazy! But I know you, I trust you, and I know you're not crazy. I've also always been aware that there is something different about you that feels deeply spiritual."

During this exchange, Vikki showed me the letters VIK all in caps and enthusiastically said, "This is my nickname. My real name is Victoria. Ask Linda, she knows!"

Linda's responded with a hearty, "Yes! Both her mother and I called her Vik and her real name is Victoria. How do you know that, Denise?"

"Vikki is able to communicate verbally with me, because I am what is known as clairaudient. In other words, I also have the ability to hear the voice of spirit as well as see and feel it." I explained.

Delighted that Linda had confirmed this young woman's name, we continued to talk about the fact that our loved ones who have traveled Home before us, are free to communicate with us. However, most times, their communications are brushed off as coincidence, nonsense, or figments of imagination and longing.

Clairvoyantly, I began to see the presence of a little boy standing next to Vikki. The angel faced child looked to be perhaps three or four years of age.

"Linda, did Vikki have a younger brother who crossed over before her?" I asked.

"Yes," she affirmed, "Vikki did have an older brother who passed on as a baby! Do you see him to?"

To help her understand, I explained that many times, an infant who has crossed over will present themselves to me as a toddler, to assist me in recognizing that they passed on as a child. It also helps me to identify if they were a boy or girl. Just as I was speaking of this phenomenon, I felt the presence of a little girl. Linda was unable to confirm whether or not Vikki also had a sister on the other side with her.

With clear communication having been established, Vikki continued to tell me about her family life.

Our dialogue continued, "Vik is talking to me about a fun loving young man who lives with her parents. His name begins with an "S", perhaps Seth or Sean. She says he's close like a brother to her. Vikki's so happy that he is taking care of her dog. It's a small, dark lap dog with really fuzzy ears. Does any of this make sense to you, Linda?"

"As a matter of fact", Linda stated, "Vikki's cousin Seth is living with her parents. Specifically, he sleeps in Vik's bedroom. And yes, Vikki's little lap dog is named, Buster."

"Denise," she continued, "this is just wild."

Throughout this exchange, our friend Cindy remained silently with us. Smiling and shedding tears right along with Linda. At one point in our conversation however, Cindy told us that she could see or sense a gold angel lapel pen. Linda and I joked that I must be rubbing off on Cindy.

When the laughter was over, Linda confirmed to both of us that at Christmas, she had gifted all of the ladies in the office with a gold angel lapel pin as a memento of just how special Vikki was to everyone. They now considered their beautiful young friend and coworker to be their guardian angel.

Cindy went on to say that she felt someone had worn their precious angel pin along their neck line. She was pleasantly surprised to learn from Linda, that Vikki's mother, Lane, had worn her golden angel treasure on the collar of her turtleneck sweater at the funeral.

Unable to let go of her vibrant young friend, Linda shared with us that she kept an angel statue on her kitchen counter at home. Vikki had a great fondness for angels. The heavenly statue reminded Marcy on a daily basis that Vik was guiding her from beyond the physical plane. It gave her peace.

The week prior to our meeting, Linda's daughter, Avery, gently placed her golden angel pin inside the mahogany jewelry box on her bedroom dresser. When Linda asked why she had done this, her daughter replied, "Because, mom, it's time to put the angel away."

"In order for you to move forward," I added, "you need to work through and let go of any guilt that you might still feel about the fact that she lost her life on the way to the office and understand that everything, including the span of our earthly existence, is in divine order."

Tearfully, Linda nodded in agreement.

Playing inside my head once more was Mariah Carey and Boys II Men. In addition, and with a big smile on her face, Vikki was singing along with them.

It was clear to me, that Vik wanted me to mention the song and find out the significance, if any.

Before I could do that however, Linda began to reflect out loud about the song SHE heard on the radio days before.

"You know," she said, "a couple of weeks ago, I was driving to work and began thinking about Vikki. All of the sudden, a song came on the radio and I just knew Vikki was sending it to me. I just can't remember the name of it though."

I chimed in, "Was it the song by Mariah Carey and Boys II Men?"

Linda's response was a jubilant, "That's the one! Yes! That's it, Denise!"

Her story continued. "I went into the office that morning and told everyone what had happened with that particular song and they treated me as if I was nuts."

"Well, you're definitely not nuts," I opined to Linda. "It also explains why I was hearing that very same song several times per week for the past few weeks and why Vikki is singing it right now."

"Have you experienced other signs?" I questioned.

"Yes," she offered, "I received a CD from my kids for Christmas that contained a song that reminds me of Vikki. It makes me cry when I listen to it."

With Vik now wearing a white lab coat, my query continued, "Has anyone else in your office experienced anything they feel is related to Vikki?"

"A few weeks after Vikki's death," she answered, "a couple of the girls had an experience in which they swore they could see Vikki's reflection in the glass door of the office."

"Did they see her wearing a white lab coat and standing just behind one of them in the reflection?" I interrupted.

Amazed at Vikki's clarity, Linda answered back, "That is exactly what they saw!"

Listening to Vikki in one ear and explaining her message to Linda, I continued, "Vikki has been trying to let all of you know that she is okay. She would like you to know that it had to happen this way. She was here for as long as she was supposed to be here. Vik wishes that everyone could understand that."

"With my third sight," I explained, "I see Vikki in an open green pasture with several beautiful horses walking about her. Along with her siblings, she is at peace and very happy to be Home. The three of them are perfectly fine."

Seeing that Linda was astounded and a bit overwhelmed by all of this, I asked her if she was alright.

"For some time now," she answered, "I've wanted to talk to someone about all of this, but didn't know who to turn to. It's not something that I felt I could talk to just anyone about. I feel much better and more peaceful now. Thank you, Denise."

Linda asked me if I would be open to talking to Vikki's mother, Lane. I told her that if it would help her in any way, I would certainly do that. I also shared that perhaps what she heard that day might also be enough to put Lane at ease.

Leaving the restaurant, Linda gave me a tearful hug and thanked me once more. "I feel like the weight of the world has been taken away from me," she softly said.

On my way home from work that evening, I asked spirit for a sign that the messages and visions that I had given Linda were on target. Instead of hearing Vikki's favorite song, the confirmation came in the form of a letter from a cousin of mine. In this letter, she described all of the good things that had come to her on the fourth day following her novena to St. Theresa. My angels had urged me to pass it along to her, after receiving the novena in the mail myself.

Knowing that angels like to hear thank you, too, I offered a hearty thanks for the signs and wonders that they help me see.

Approximately two weeks later, Linda phoned me. She told me how much better she felt since our conversation and to let me know that she had spoken with Vikki's mother, Lane.

"Lane was amazed by what you told me Denise. She would love to be able to speak with you. Would you be open to that?" she asked.

My response was one of knowing that God had something special in mind for this meeting. "Yes, of course. I would be happy to, Linda," was my reply.

"Oh," Linda went on to say, "you were right about the children with Vikki, Denise. Her parents also lost a little girl as well as the little boy. Lane was so relieved to know that her three children are all together and happily at peace."

It's an indescribable feeling to know that I was able to help Vikki's mother in some small way. The mere thought of losing one of my own children, brings such anguish, that I cannot possibly imagine what it feels like to have that be a reality. A reality that Vikki's mother had experienced not once, but three times.

Early one morning toward the end of April, Linda called to ask me if I would meet her and Vikki's mother for lunch on the following day. With spring in the air and the ground beginning to thaw, Vikki's mother wanted to speak to me because the graveside burial and interment service for her daughter was going to take place at the end of that very week. Lane hoped that meeting with me would help her through the task of burying yet another child.

I agreed to meet with them for lunch the next day.

Hanging up the phone, I asked for God's guidance and strength. Because I had never met either Vikki or her mother, I was a bit nervous. Although Linda assured me that Lane was completely open to spiritual phenomena, I was still a bit worried that I might make an error in my interpretation and harm, rather than help this woman.

Sitting alone for a moment, in a quite space, I immediately felt Vikki's vibrant presence. Beginning with a lovely Christian baptismal gown, white with a pink bow or flower on the bodice, she began to show me a series of items that were relevant to her life. Next was a cedar chest of cherry or mahogany, followed by what appeared to be a woman's white dress, and finally a light colored casket.

Holding out her right hand, Vikki showed me an exquisite St. Mary's Miraculous Medal made of gold. Its reverse side was resplendent with an engraving of the Sacred Heart of Jesus.

In her left she held a lovely Catholic rosary. While doing so, Vikki repeated the word, "Carmelite" out loud to me. I wondered if perhaps Vikki was devout to the Blessed Mother, Mary, or if she attended a church named after this beloved saint. There was a meaning to the rosary and miraculous medal. One that I was destined to discover.

Later that afternoon, I phoned Linda to confirm our lunch plans.

During our brief conversation, I asked her if Vikki's casket was white and if she had been laid to rest wearing white clothing adorned with pink roses. While she could not recall the color of Vikki's casket, she did remember that her young friend was wearing a white sweater and a wrist corsage of tiny pink roses.

Feeling compelled to know further details, I asked, "Is she holding a rosary in her left hand, Linda?"

Linda clearly remembered that Vikki's mother had definitely placed the rosary in her daughter's hand, before funeral home visitations began.

Pressing on, I inquired, "What about an association with St. Mary? Perhaps it was a church she attended? Or did she actually wear a shiny gold Miraculous Medal?"

"I'm not certain about that," was her quick reply.

With that, I expressed to Linda that I felt Vikki's father was not dealing with her death as well as her mother had been. Linda confirmed my feeling by telling me that for a very long time following Vikki's passing, her father would not speak to people, or leave their family home.

Having affirmed my intuition, I thanked Linda and told her I looked forward to seeing her and Lane at lunch the next day...

Sitting directly across from me was a mother who had endured not once, but three times, a grief that very few experience and of those who do, many do not survive.

Her lovely eyes and sunny disposition were the very first things that I noticed about Lane, as she sat down to join us around the bistro table. What caught my eyes next was the gold St. Mary's Miraculous Medal that she was wearing around her neck.

"It belonged to Vikki," was her response when I told her that Vikki had shown me the very same medal only a day before.

When I asked Lane about the Catholic rosary that Vikki had been holding in her hand, she explained to Linda and me that they had been a gift from Vik's Godmother. Lane wanted her daughter to carry them with her to her heavenly home.

Lane and I spoke about Vikki's outgoing personality. As we talked, she pulled a senior high school photo from her wallet. Just as I had seen so many times before, Vik's now familiar face was decorated with a big, bright smile from ear to ear.

"I get the sense that Vikki loved the outdoors, Lane. She continues to show me a pastoral scene in which she is sitting on a fence, facing forward, with a look of peaceful joy in her eyes." Continuing on, I asked, "Does this describe Vikki in any way?"

"Vikki loved the outdoors!" was Lane's impassioned reply.

"In fact," she continued, "I'd like to show you something that I brought with me today." Reaching into her purse, Lane pulled out several photos and placed one in particular directly in front of me. Complete with a pastoral background, it was a snapshot of Vikki sitting on a stone fence. Her pose was the identical stance that I had seen clairvoyantly on so many previous occasions.

The subsequent photo showed Vikki with her brown and white spotted, cocker spaniel dog, Max.

"Did Vikki have another dog? Specifically, a small dark colored lap dog with fuzzy face and ears?" I asked.

With a hardy laugh, Lane said, "Yes! You just described her miniature schnauzer, Buster!

"He died just a little over a year ago," she explained. "Vikki was heartbroken at the time. Are you telling me that they are together now?"

With a smile in my heart I replied, "Yes, that's what I'm telling you, Lane."

The mood on Lane's face then went from joyful to somber when she asked the following question, "Tell me Denise, why doesn't Vikki come to me? Why does she come to visit you and not me? After all, I'm her mother."

The pain in her voice was nearly palpable and the tears brimming in her eyes told me that this was something weighed heavily on Lane's heart.

Linda spoke up at this point and said to Lane, "Perhaps it's because you are looking too hard for the obvious signs of her presence. Maybe," she elaborated, "you need to pay attention to the more subtle signs of her presence."

Offering a view that might help, I added, "When you think about it Lane, if Vikki had not come to me at lunch several weeks ago, Linda might not have experienced any of this. As part of her healing process, Linda needed to hear these things for herself in order to move forward." This explanation made Lane smile.

"That makes perfect sense," Lane replied. "It's just that I want to see her so badly, though."

"Once you stop looking so hard," I told Lane, "there is no doubt in my mind that you will see or feel her presence. Surely, you must have had at least one or two instances up until now, that have made you think that Vikki was near."

Lane admitted that during the winter months she'd had the unexplainable feeling that Vikki was going to die. On the morning of the accident that claimed her daughter's life, Lane was driving to work with a friend, when she heard news of an awful traffic accident. In her heart Lane hoped that they were not talking about her only daughter. Something else told her however, that they were.

Not long after arriving at her office, Lane received the phone call that is every parent's worst nightmare. She had been summoned to the local hospital, where her daughter's physical body lay lifeless.

Clairsentiently, I could fee that Vikki suffered severe trauma to her chest area. Her face however, felt as though it was perfectly, beautifully intact. When I relayed this feeling to her mother, Lane confirmed this by sharing with me that by looking at Vikki's face, you would not have known that she had been injured. She had no head trauma. However, the damage to her chest area was severe enough that one of her breasts was literally torn away from her body.

Our conversation continued on when I began to ask about the baptismal gown. "Why does Vikki show me a beautiful white baptismal gown, Lane? She tells me that it's stored in the cedar chest. Any idea why she keeps bringing it to my attention?"

From the look on her face, I could tell that this subject was an emotional one for Lane.

"Yes, Denise," she answered, "Vik's baptismal gown is in the cedar chest. I've been wondering lately, what to do with it. A very dear friend of my daughter has asked me if she might be able to have her newborn child baptized wearing Vikki's gown. I told her that she is welcome to do so, but I can't seem to muster up the courage to open the cedar chest and take it out. I'm afraid of the memories, and I'm afraid that Vik would not approve."

Within my 'inner' ear, I could hear Vikki respond with an emphatic, "Yes! By all means, let her use it!"

A smile appeared on Lane's face as I relayed this message from her daughter and she began to discuss Vikki's jewelry.

I asked Lane if Vikki owned a high school class ring. "No," she said, "Vik didn't want to waste money on something that she felt she wouldn't actually wear. She was practical like that."

Despite her mother's response to the contrary, Vikki was persistent in showing me a sterling silver, dome shaped class ring that was set with a dark blue sapphire colored stone.

When those in spirit are unceasing in their attempt to deliver a significant message, I've found it valuable to investigate further. I did just that when I asked, Lane if Vikki had a boyfriend who might have worn such a ring.

"Oh my God, Denise, yes!" was her fervent reply. Her boyfriend owns this ring! He gave it to her to wear while they were dating. I just gave it back a few weeks ago! That is unbelievable."

Noticing the Immaculate Heart symbol that was engraved on the back side of Lane's gold pendant, I inquired as to which church Vikki attended on a regular basis. With a tone of curiosity she replied, "Together, she and her grandmother attended St. Anthony's every Sunday. Why?"

Lane's face lit up with excitement, as I described how Vikki had given me the impression that she had a significant tie to a church dedicated to the Blessed Mother.

Her excitement was explained, when Lane shared with me that Vikki had received the Catholic Sacrament of Confirmation at St. Mary's Church.

At this point in our conversation, I could clearly see that Vikki was standing behind the mother that she so dearly loved. Her arms were hugging Lane around the neck, as she gave her a gentle kiss on the cheek.

Describing this scene of affection, brought fresh tears to Lane's face as she told me how often her daughter hugged and kissed her; and just how often Vikki told her mom how much she loved her.

"I told her just a few weeks before she died, that I didn't know what I would do without her, Denise. Does she miss me, too?"

Repeating what Vik was now saying, I said, "She misses you, too, Lane. But she also wants you to know that she is always with you."

Desperation filled Lane's voice as her questions continued. "Does it hurt her when I cry? Does it prohibit her from moving on?"

Gently, I replied, "No, Lane. She understands your tears, and your love for her in no way prevents her from moving on. Our souls are vast, they are eternal, and they are always connected to those we love."

The presence of a paternal grandmother and that of godfather were with Vikki. The woman assured me that all three of Lane's children were with her and were well. Lane acknowledged that prior to Vikki's passing, she gave birth to a son that was stillborn and delivered a daughter that died shortly after birth. Lane felt relief in knowing that her children were all together and at peace in the Heavenly realm of love.

Lane spent much of the remainder of our time together, reminiscing about her golden haired daughter; the light of her life. She asked me if I thought we each had a certain amount of time dedicated to living on earth or if we die simply by accident.

My belief has always been that each of us comes to the earth plane to accomplish our souls' unique mission. For some, I explained, the soul assignment is accomplished in a few living moments, while for others, decades are required. Ultimately, I believe, we are here no longer than the time it takes to make our loving difference in the world.

Linda added to this conversation by saying that she felt Vikki's time was so brief by human standards because she accomplished so much and touched so many lives in such a short amount of time.

A homeless man had been living behind the office building that Linda and Vikki worked in. Each day during her lunch break, Vik would bring food to this man. During the colder months, she brought this gentleman a warm, winter coat.

"When I told Vik to be careful of him, she wouldn't listen." In a low, tear filled voice Linda went on to say, "The strange thing is, as soon as Vikki passed away, we never saw the homeless man again."

"When I was naked, you clothed me. When I was hungry you fed me." These words played round and round in my mind as I took within me, the spiritual significance of what Linda had just shared.

More than just feeding and clothing a homeless man, Vikki truly lived the words she heard spoken each Sunday at Mass.

Asking Lane about Vikki's father revealed a man who was yet unable to cope with the death of his daughter. She confirmed that his days were spent in his blue reclining chair, gazing endlessly into the void of his television. With Vikki's photo squarely placed upon the small table at his side, his days were filled with mind numbing talk shows and paid programming.

Staring wistfully out of the restaurant window, Lane spoke. "Her father needs closure. Perhaps the beginning of that will come after the burial service on Friday. I pray this is so."

As we prepared to leave the café, I expressed to Lane that it had been my pleasure to meet her, but that I wished it had been under happier circumstances.

"I know we'll see each other again," she said.

As I gave her a hug, I told Lane that I would like that.

Walking through the restaurant doors, we chuckled once more about how Lane had expected me to be a shriveled old woman with a crystal ball, and how relieved she was to find me quite ordinary, if not a bit plain.

That day, I was taught about the strength of faith in the face of insurmountable grief. It is a lesson that I have not forgotten and a gift from Lane and Vikki that I shall always cherish.

"Let nothing dim the
Light that shines
from within."

-Maya Angelou

"Lois and the Archangel St. Raphael"

The following account of Angelic intervention was written by the recipient of this Divine blessing, in her own words:

When my granddaughter told me she wanted to talk to me, I was like most grandmothers with teenage grandchildren. I thought our conversation would be about another boy problem or the hatching of some new teenage plan on the horizon.

My assumption was horribly wrong and I was not prepared to hear what my eldest granddaughter had to tell me; she was suffering with a serious health issue. As our conversation came to an end, I gave her all the hugs that I possibly could while she was still in my house and within arms reach. My tears of anguish were saved for when she left and could no longer see my face. Thinking about life without my free spirited granddaughter was more than my mind or heart could bear.

During the weeks following our heart to heart talk, my grandchild went through a continuous battery of painful medical testing and the anxious waiting. During the course of this process, I learned that I, too, had a life threatening health issue. A woman's worst nightmare was beginning to take form in my life.

Years of normal mammograms came to a screeching halt, revealing a large abnormality in my breast tissue. Hearing this news brought very frightening thoughts to my mind. Despite my fear, however, my physician did not seem concerned and scheduled me for a biopsy. The two weeks that I would have to wait felt like an eternity.

Had it not been for an extensive family history that includes so much cancer, I know I would have been able to gather up a more positive attitude. However, knowing that so many of my own family members had succumbed to cancer, I found myself talking to my Angels every night, as I lie in bed.

When I first began praying with the Angels nearly two years ago, they always let me know they were with me by revealing beautiful flashes of colorful, undulating light behind my closed eyes. The unearthly and indescribable colors of these Angelic encounters left me knowing for certain, that I was not alone. The celestial colors brought with them a sense of peace and a calm knowing that God was with me.

The Archangel St. Michael comes to me with the gift of indigo blue lights dancing across my inner vision. Along with this heavenly sign, he also brings relaxation and a sense that I am divinely protected. Fearing my upcoming biopsy, St. Michael's visits provided a respite from the constant anxiety.

Following the conversation with my granddaughter, prayers for the safe return of her health began in earnest. On one particular evening, as I lay in bed having a conversation with the Archangel St. Raphael, the Angel of healing, I had a life altering experience of the heavenly kind. Wrapping up my prayers with my usual amen, I gently opened my eyes.

To my great surprise, I saw before me, a picture of the Great Pyramid framed in oak. The apparition appeared to be hanging on the wall directly in front me. Although it hung there for only a few seconds, it was long enough for me to recognize that this was a positive sign. I learned long ago that the Great Pyramid of Giza not only represents one of the Wonders of the World, but also represents healing and sacred prayer. Positive thoughts welcomed my sleep that night. Something from deep within me told me that everything was going to be okay.

Two nights later, I was once again in deep conversation with my Angels. I don't know why I had so much fear this night, after encountering the specter of the Pyramid only a couple of nights earlier. In my prayers, I told my Angels how afraid I was and asked for their help to get me through all of the testing that would soon take place for both my granddaughter and me. For some reason, I opened my eyes during my prayers, turned my head to the right and before me was a face. The stark apparition startled and surprised me.

In the very short time that the ghostly face was clearly visible to me, I was able to memorize all of the features of this face. It was as though my brain took a photograph of this visage and stored it in my memory.

The next morning, I told my husband about the face that appeared to me during my prayers for healing. Describing the stubble and whiskers, the surgical mask and self assured look, my husband told me that he felt I was describing Dr. House, a fictional television character from the weekly show called, "House". As a fan of the show, I often told my husband that if I ever had a serious health issue, I would want a Dr. House in real life. Despite his poor bedside manner, the character, Dr. House, was known as the best in the business and a doc that could solve any medical mystery with a positive outcome.

Before long, the day finally came for me to visit my doctor for a surgical biopsy. To my surprise, the physician that I was assigned to was the one I had on my very first visit for a medical assessment. Knowing that this particular doctor was the very same one who didn't seem concerned about my condition, I felt a sense of relief.

That sense of relief was quickly replaced with frustration when I asked a few simple questions of him as I was prepared for surgery. Like the TV character, my surgeon shared the same lack of bedside manner as the fictional Dr. House. My questions were met with very stern and abrupt one word answers. Before long, I was wheeled in to surgery, never to see the surgeon again.

The process of waiting for the biopsy results began and my nightly conversations with my Angels continued on.

Within days, we learned that everything had turned out well for my granddaughter. Her condition was under control and the outlook for recovery looked good. Shortly following her good news, I received welcome news of my own.

Through this experience, I have come to realize that Angels really are there for us when you ask for their assistance, and even when you don't. In my life, my Angelic guardians kept trying over and over to get through to me, but I wouldn't see their presence in my life. Finally, my prayers were answered when they appeared to me with a human-like vision that I would understand. In this case, it was a hardnosed surgeon with no bedside manner but one who knows his business as a healer. I asked the Angels to lead me to a Dr. House, and a Dr. House is exactly what I was given.

I know beyond a doubt that everything happens for a reason. The Angels know when you need them and they will come to your rescue in many ways. Knowing this and truly believing it gives me great comfort and courage to face whatever may come in the future.

Angels truly are among us.

"…that the best portion of a good man's life,
his little, nameless, unremembered acts of
kindness and love."

-William Wordsworth

"Nick and the Wooden Rosary"

Some of my very favorite individuals are what I call, "shooting stars." Shooting stars are beautiful young people who come into this world and blaze an enormous trail of good works, brilliant ideas, acts of random kindness, and all around love. They are much older than their physical years reflect, and greatly wiser than their formal education may imply.

If there is a way of defining an Earth Angel, to me, shooting stars apply.

There's only one problem with shooting stars, however. You see, shooting stars, to the human mind, are young people who have gone Home far too soon. To the God mind, there is an understanding that their youthful star blazed for as long as it was supposed to, and at the end of its brief earthly cycle, it was awarded the gift of going Home to celebrate their numerous, selfless accomplishments.

Our God heart understands this concept, our human heart grieves it.

The crisp autumn air of 2008 brought with it, a vivacious shooting star named Nick. It also brought a brokenhearted mother named Patricia into my home and into my life. It was a divine encounter that I am certain I shall never forget.

Before I ever opened the door to greet Nick's lovely, brown-eyed, and raven-haired mother, her tall and lanky teenage son, sporting a wavy mop of auburn hair, woke me from my sleep that particular morning.

Barely past the wee hour of 6:00 a.m., prior to my eyes even thinking of opening to greet the day, I heard a young man's voice say with great enthusiasm, "Denise, it's time to get up. Come on, my mom's gonna be here soon. You need to get up!"

Apparently noticing that my physical body was still somewhat in the dream state, Nick took his morning salutation a step further. With a gentle poke on my right shoulder, my eyes sprang open wide to comprehend the figure of a vibrant teenager whom I guessed was approximately 18 years of age. A broad and dazzling smile adorned his handsome young face.

Pulling the warm covers aside of my body and checking the bedroom alarm clock for the time, Nick told me that his mother was coming to see me and that he had a whole bunch that he would like to say to her.

Right out loud, I gently assured him that he could tell her all that he felt he needed to and more, but that in the meantime, I needed to prepare for my day. With the flash of another broad smile, Nick left my sight, but it was very clear that his delightful energy was still around me. Part of me chuckled at the sheer joy that emanated from such a radiant soul yet a part of me felt deep sadness for the woman who had given him birth.

Without ever telling my assistant why she was booking a private reading session with me, Patricia was hopeful that I would be able to connect with her only son, who had gone Home only months earlier.

Nick would make sure that her hope would be fulfilled.

Hours after my morning wake up call and with his grieving mother now sitting directly across from me, the veil between the physical and non physical worlds was parted and Nick made a wonderfully grand entrance into the room.

As we settled into the room and became acquainted, I began telling Patricia about the course of my morning and my interaction with her son, Nick.

Her eyes welled up with stinging tears that began to course down her cheeks. These were the very same cheeks that Nick had kissed a thousand times during his stay on earth; affectionate and playful kisses that were sorely missed by his loving mother and father.

After describing her son in the manner in which I saw him, Patricia pulled from her leather purse, a photo of her smiling, energetic son. Staring back at me from the glossy photo was the gregarious face of the teenager who had awakened me from my slumber hours earlier. A smile couldn't help but spread across my face.

Although our three way conversation lasted for a full sixty minutes; some parts delightfully happy and others dreadfully sad, there was a particular point in the conversation that has become a treasure to Nick's parents, to the countless numbers that I have recounted it to, and to me.

Three quarters of the way through our allotted time, Nick held out his right hand and presented before me what appeared to be a large wooden rosary.

Telepathically, I asked him what it meant.

"I'm giving it to my mom." was his immediate response. "She'll understand in a few days, Denise. Just tell her what it is I'm giving her."

Not quite certain where to begin, I described in detail the scene before me to Patricia.

When she responded by telling me that she was not Catholic, nor was Nick, I assured her that although this sign from him did make sense in the present moment, it would become a clear sign of Nick's presence in the very near future.

Neither the vision of Nick holding the wooden rosary or my subsequent explanation made much sense to Patricia. She took note of it, however, and thanked me for the message.

When our time together wrapped up, Patricia hugged me tightly and shared her appreciation for my ability to connect with Nick. With the holidays in full bloom, I gently reminded her that Nick had asked that she and her husband not forgo decorating a Christmas tree. It was after all, one of his favorite holidays and a day that he would, of course, spend with them from his home in Love. Patricia smiled a tearful smile and made her way back to her car, which was parked just a few feet from my front door.

I spent a great deal of time that particular Saturday, thinking about Patricia, her husband Joe, and their outgoing son, Nick. Within the span of 17 years he became a martial artist, played and coached youth lacrosse, refereed at lacrosse sporting events, volunteered at a local senior center, befriended people from all walks of life, mentored young boys, and volunteered to be the permanent designated driver to his fellow high school classmates, who might sometime need a sober ride home in the middle of the night.

Generous at helping others was common for Nick. In doing so, it would be his pledge to be a sober driver for friends in need that eventually cost him his physical life. It was while driving a classmate home from a party he had not himself attended, Nick was killed in a car crash only miles from home. His passenger survived.

My Catholic upbringing makes me think of prayer when I see a holy rosary. It makes me think of prayers to the Mother and the prayers of a mother. Some believe that the prayers of a mother are the strongest and most loudly heard in heaven. Perhaps it was a combination of Patricia's prayers and Nick's determination to answer his mother's prayers that lead to the miracle that occurred only two days after our meeting.

The email that I received from Patricia the following Tuesday morning is truly unforgettable. In it, she recounted the amazing events that took place as she was leaving work on the evening prior. As she and a coworker trudged across the snow filled parking lot of their employer, the co-worker said, "Patricia, didn't Denise tell you that Nick wanted you and Joe to put a Christmas tree up this year?"

Sadly she replied, "Yes, he did. But we really don't feel like it."

Pointing to the Christmas tree vendor that was stationed in the far corner of the company parking lot, her friend continued, "Come on Pat, why don't we at least go and take a look at the trees. I think Nick would like that."

Patricia agreed and the two of them began the trek toward the brightly lit Christmas tree stand before them.

What happened in the very short distance between the office and the tree stand is to me, proof of the unending love that mystic poets write about and Angels continually talk about.

With his finger pointing toward a group of nearly empty parking spaces, Patricia's coworker said, "Pat, what is that hanging on the handicapped parking sign right there?"

Without interest in what he was talking about, she said, "I don't know. Let's keep going."

Insisting that they discover what it was that was hanging from the sign, her friend lead her right up to what I deem a treasure from heaven. There, right before them, hanging from a blue handicap parking sign, was a large brown, wooden rosary!

Carefully removing it from its precarious perch, Patricia could hardly believe her eyes. Her mind told her it was impossible, but her mother's heart knew otherwise.

"Could it be?" she thought.

"Of course it is," her son would reply.

Directly in front of her unbelieving eyes, was the rosary, made of rich mahogany wood.

Gingerly removing it from its place upon the sign, it was difficult for Patricia to grasp the magnitude of what she was now experiencing.

With the help of Angels, Nick had helped his mother and her coworker experience firsthand, the power of eternal love. Not only can it help to move mountains, eternal love can move us out of the darkness of grief and into the Light of understanding.

It was on a subsequent visit to my home, with the wooden rosary in tow, that I met Patricia's husband and Nick's father, Joe.

A gentle man with soft eyes and a father's unconditional heart entered my house and embraced me. Not quite sure what to make of the events surrounding the previous meeting with his wife, or the discovery of the rosary, he was at the very least, willing to listen to what I and/or his son might have to say in the coming hour.

Within moments of having me hold the rosary, Nick was present with us in the room and ready to speak to the man that he loved most of all; his devoted father.

Without hesitation, Nick launched into a conversation about how he loved riding on a jet ski, working on cars together with his dad, and his pride at having a father who was now mentoring a young man in becoming a referee in his favorite sport of lacrosse.

It was when Nick unexpectedly began to sing "Happy Birthday" to his father that Joe came to know that it was indeed his son, who was speaking through me. Neither he nor Patricia had let that proverbial cat out of the bag, and only one other person would know it was Joe's birthday weekend.

In the many months since our first sessions together, Nick has let his father and mother know that he is well aware of life happenings on this side of the veil. From recognizing the memorial lacrosse tournament that now bears his name, to the honoring of his jersey, and even the bull mastiff puppy that one his friends had come to own.

Is it that our loved ones in spirit are bored with nothing to do, and so they spend their heavenly time coming up with ways to connect with us, or is it their desire to help us heal and to let us know they are still quite alive that prompts their interactions? I believe it's the latter that best explains this phenomenon.

The same might be asked of the Angels who intervene on our behalf in sometimes extravagant ways.

*"Come with us into the heavenly garden and walk
with the brethren of the light. Commune with the
angelic company. Angels are unmoved by passion.
They appear to be without emotion because they are
emotionally still and disciplined. They live in the aura,
the consciousness, the life of divine Mother, and in the
infinite and eternal garden you will see angelic forces
in colours unmatched on earth, still and peaceful,
continually giving, giving, giving help; pouring love
and wisdom upon creation."*

-White Eagle
"Walking with the Angels"

The Angel and the Missing iPhone

Take the case of 17 year old Elyse. Only two weeks away from high school graduation and feeling confident about her long term future, it was her short term dilemma that dampened her spirits.

It was a Monday morning like any other for a high school senior who was wrapping up 13 years of formal education. Year end exams had come to an end and the lazy days of May were upon her.

That was, until first hour arrived and her good friend James asked her if she had, as promised, downloaded new songs on his iPhone. The tunes she had agreed to add to his phone collection only three days earlier.

Reaching into her designer purse and scouring its many fabric lined compartments for James phone, she came up empty handed. Certain that the phone must be within the confines of her shoulder bag, she meticulously emptied its contents on her classroom desk. James' brand new phone was nowhere to be found.

Elyse explained to James that she was certain that his phone was either left inside her car or still in her bedroom near her laptop computer. In any event, she would look in both places and return it to him right away.

Within minutes, her automobile insides had been turned inside out. She looked in every crevice, under every floor mat, as panic began to set in. With no phone to be found, she started her Mercury Cougar and headed for home.

With trembling fingers dialing the numbers on the keypad and a trembling voice speaking through her own phone, she dialed her mom.

Hearing my daughter's quivering voice on my phone, I knew in an instant that something was amiss. After explaining her dilemma to me, and asking me to use my 'psychic powers' to find the missing object, I explained to my free spirited daughter that in this instance, she needed to ask the Angels for help.

"Take a deep breath and call in the help of your Guardian Angels," I advised. "Be sure to call me when it's found," I continued, "and to thank your Angels for helping you find it!"

Ten minutes later I received a subsequent phone call from my forlorn daughter, proclaiming that every inch of her bedroom had been overturned, that her car had been turned inside out, and that her purse had been emptied of all its contents and yet, no hint of James' phone had been found.

Once again, I advised my youngest child to ask her Guardian Angels for help and told her that it was time to be open to miracles. Something or someone had let me know that one was on its way. A heavenly form of a high school graduation gift was in store for Elyse.

With sadness in her voice, she hung up the phone. With hope in her heart, she began to ask more earnestly than ever, for divine intervention.

Perhaps it was four minutes later, her phone rang. It was James.

A young man with surprise in his voice and delight in his demeanor greeted my daughter with, "Elyse, how did you manage to put my phone back in my pocket without me knowing? I haven't seen you since we talked earlier! How did you do that? I reached into my pocket for money and found my phone instead! Did you sneak up on me without me being aware?"

Rather than answer his question directly, Elyse simply laughed and told him it was a secret.

When she relayed the conversation to me, she wanted to know how that 'secret' had actually happened!

"You asked the Angels for help, didn't you?" I answered.

"No, I didn't ask. I begged!!!" was her flabbergasted response.

"But mom," she continued, "how does that happen? How does a phone suddenly appear out of thin air and into someone's jeans pocket? I'm serious, mom, how does that happen?"

Over the course of her nearly 18 years I had talked to her many times about the reality of miracles and divine intervention. I stopped to silently thank the Angels for giving my child a heavenly Gift that she would not ever forget and one that would give her life an expanded awareness of God.

"Seriously mom," she countered, "James wants to know how I did it! What am I going to tell him?" she inquired.

Chuckling out loud, I responded, "I will leave that answer up to you and your team of intrepid Angels, Elyse. I'm certain that all of you will come up with an explanation that will be just perfect for this occasion."

Although I couldn't see it, I knew my answer had been met with a teenage eyeball roll that was balanced with a heart full of relief and a mind filled with wonder.

"Happy graduation, my love!" Those were my final words as our conversation came to a happy end.

"I am one with all of Nature.
I am one with Mother Earth."

-Ariel, Archangel of the Animal Kingdom

An Angel Named Echo

Just when I thought the 7th chapter of this book was complete my heavenly guides corrected me by tossing the following question at me: "Dana, what about the work we do with animals? You've not mentioned anything about animals and their guardian Angels, or animals that do Angelic work on earth and animals who are actually Angels in disguise. We feel it's important that you include a few words about this topic."

"You know what?" I offered. "You're right and I know someone very special who might have a story or two to share about this exciting subject matter."

With glee in their voices and what appeared to be extra sparkles in their halos, I heard them give a hearty, "Thanks, Dana! You're right. Jeanna is perfect for the job! We appreciate you both."

As the human mother of two paint horses named Tussy and Beau, a Yorkshire Terrier named Merlin, and a Jack Russell Terrier named Gabriel James, I have to admit, they often remind me that Angels can also wear feathers, fur, fins, and sometimes even…scales.

Here enters my dear friend from southern Indiana, Jeanna.

When I first met this gentle soul with a charming southern drawl in 2004, I immediately became aware of her Gift. Jeanna has the profound ability to communicate with the animal kingdom. Fondly, I call her the insect and animal whisperer.

Together, we have journeyed to England, Mount Shasta, and twice to Egypt. Nepal is next on the list. Travel photos will attest to the fact that even the crabbiest of camels on the Giza Plateau, homeless dogs at The Red Pyramid, our feathered friends on Mount Shasta, and at Merlin's Cave in Tintagel, love this woman. Whether it's her animal friends at the Humane Society she volunteers at, the ones she meets on a regular basis at various pet rescues and shelters, or her very own menagerie at home, it is clearly obvious that Jeanna loves them, too.

When I told her that the Angels suggested she might have a story to contribute to this book and asked her if she might be willing to do so, she quickly agreed and knew just the story she wanted to share:

It was a difficult time for our family. Our beloved mini-dachshund, Rowdy, had become seriously ill. His shining mahogany red coat grew dull, once sparkling eyes were lackluster. Our perpetual motion puppy was not interested in anything except lying listlessly on the sofa. Perhaps most upsetting was that all Rowdy's medical tests came back as normal. We were at a loss. When questioned, Rowdy could only say that he thought he was dying.

Since recently learning the ancient energy healing method known as Reiki, I thought maybe that would be of some benefit and so began daily treatments to the little fellow. On one of Rowdy's particularly bad days, I looked skyward and said, "Is anybody up there? We sure could use some help right about now, how about a guardian angel—do animals have angels—does Rowdy have one?"

Was I ever surprised when a gentle voice replied, "Rowdy has a guardian angel, my name is Echo." Rowdy cocked his head and listened intently. "Did you hear that," I asked? He affirmed that he did indeed hear the angelic reply and promptly went to sleep.

The very next day, my skeptical self began questioning the validity of angelic communication. Did animals have guardian angels? Or was my imagination just really active? While pondering these questions, Rowdy indicated that he was ready for a Reiki session. Tuning the television to a station playing peaceful, soothing music, we began the energy work. All of a sudden, the television went completely silent. Glancing up, I saw these words emblazoned across the bright green screen—

"ECHO IS HERE"

Yes, animals have guardian angels. We need only be open to their presence. Echo remained in our lives as Rowdy's angel for the many happy years he was with us, a loving presence, a guiding Spirit for a little red dachshund with a heart as big as the world.

"Animals are unpredictable things, and so our life is unpredictable. It's a long tale of little triumphs and disasters and you've got to really like it to stick to it."

-James Herriot (1890 – 1960), veterinary surgeon and author of
"All Creatures Great and Small."

"Then I said to him:
'Lord, when someone meets you
In a Moment of vision,
Is it through the soul (psyche) that they see,
Or is it through the Spirit (Pneuma)?'
The Teacher answered:
'It is neither through the soul nor the spirit,
But the nous between the two
Which sees the vision, and it is this which...'
-Mary Magdalene
"The Gospel of Mary Magdalene"

The Mystic's Angel

It has often been said, and I heartily agree, that sacred wisdom is not given, it is earned by the soul that is ready to wield it in a positive, loving manner. We are after all, responsible for the knowledge that we acquire and the way in which we use it.

There are souls who arrive on the earth plane already working on their master's degree in the proper use of the charismata, also known as the gifts of spirit. They are born seeing, sensing, hearing, and tasting the realm of Spirit. These are mystical adepts in the making.

Others arrive in a state of forgetfulness that renders them a student in what I call spiritual kindergarten. These are the novices who are beginning to hear the calling of their soul. They can no longer ignore the promptings of their spirit and are working their way toward becoming a spiritual initiate. Much like Dorothy, they are starting to walk the supernatural, yellow brick road.

Between both of those places, we find millions of adventurous souls who are fully embracing their divinity and working toward self mastery of body, mind, and spirit.

As with any person who is working on perfecting their personal and professional talents, there are steps involved in attaining mastery of them. Whether it is through a vocational education, college, apprenticeship, or the school of hard knocks, everyone goes through a sequential process of gaining knowledge in order to graduate in their chosen field.

A mystic's journey is no different than that of a doctor or a plumber; except to say, that part of their schooling happens while the physical body is fast asleep. Within the nocturnal world of dreams, the spirit body awakens and encounters an academy for divine, angelic interaction and Higher education.

The mystic whose feet are planted firmly on the path of spirit, encounters a dream-time team of Angelic guides who lead them in the proper progression of their spiritual course. Oftentimes, these encounters during sleep will increase in intensity and frequency at the point in which a spiritual graduation is at hand.

Inner plane mystery schools are found in the nous. That place between the non-physical and physical realms. These are the institutions of higher education that the mystic enrolls in prior to physical incarnation. Acceptance into the program is received after birth when the incarnated soul agrees to walk the path of spirit that it has chosen.

Formal acceptance into the Modern Day Mystic curriculum came to me in 1994. Seven nights per week found me in the classroom of my interior castle, waging war with those things in my life, such as fear, that needed to be released, in order for me to move forward on my soul's chosen path. During my waking hours, I had already begun in earnest, the process of becoming a student of the esoteric or hidden wisdom offered by the Christian Gnostics, Church mystics, and that of the Hebrew Kabbalists.

St. Teresa of Avila, the 16th century Spanish mystic, wrote often and profusely about the interior castle of the soul; the many mansions of God within. The words of this humble saint, remind us all that it is within our interior castle that we meet our divine self, the Angels, and of course, the One who loves us most of all.

Slipping into the landscape of my dreamtime, I arrived each night well within the interior castle of my psyche, and into a stark stone walled room that was menacing, dark, and gray. Sweat pouring from my brow and a constant cadence of prayers streaming from my lips, I encountered what I called, "The Troll."

For lack of a better description, my dreamtime nemesis, with unruly bushy black hair, broad face, and sinewy arms appeared half cave man, half troll. He was mean. He intended to kill me, of that I was certain. The Troll wanted me to die.

In addition to having a nasty comportment, he sported a full length sword of what appeared to be dull platinum. It was with this sword that he matched his dueling skills with mine, each and every night. During those seemingly endless hours, Hail Mary's filled the unseen halls of my interior castle and the four walls of my bedroom at home. The Holy Mother had always been a constant source of solace for me. I was certain that she would also be my source of strength and protection, as I fought to stay alive.

To describe myself as being tired upon waking each morning, is a gross understatement. It didn't take long before physical, mental, and spiritual exhaustion began to settle over me. Despite my attempts to pray the nightmare away before bedtime, the dreams continued. The Troll would not give up his quest to destroy my Light.

In the darkness of a cold November night that very same year, the fighting finally ceased.

Face to face once again with The Troll, and with my faithful metal sword nowhere to be found, as if by magic, a brand new, shinier sword was tossed to me by a pair of unseen hands.

With a single movement, I silently raised my glistening new sword and promptly lobbed off The Trolls revolting head. The Trolls dying body swayed back and forth until it crumpled to the floor, sitting lotus style in front of me. Its hideous head was somewhere near the now lifeless body. The Troll was dead.

Hardly believing what was directly before my eyes, I felt both sorrow and a wave of utter relief. Like The Troll, I dropped to the floor, and with my sword gently lying across my lap, I stared at the scene in front of me.

As I took in the sights and smells all around my dream, the head of The Troll began to roll across the floor, until ultimately it was facing upward and grimacing at me from its resting place in my lap. In total disgust, I rolled The Trolls head back toward the headless body that was still sitting only a few feet in front of me. I watched with utter amazement as the gnarly, lifeless hands of The Troll reached for its decapitated head and promptly placed it back where it belonged.

Before I could raise my brilliant sword from my lap and posture myself for yet another defense, I became witness to something that in a moment of grace has altered my interior life and the physical life that I lead on earth.

In one fluid motion, the being that I had come to call The Troll, stood up and transformed itself into the most radiant Angelic being I have ever seen. The sound of its glorious, luminescent wings unfurling is one that to this day, brings delight to my soul.

The indescribable radiance of the Archangel St. Michael now stood where there once stood a troll. The aura of celestial Light that emanated from his being, filled the entirety of my interior castle and brought unspeakable joy to my soul.

Drawing his crystalline sword upright toward his shimmering torso, my guardian Angel of Light spoke to me.

"Congratulations, Dana. You have won the battle. Your willingness to bring Light to darkened places is applauded by the Heavenly host and the fullness of your spiritual Journey is now at hand. Go forth on the path of your soul knowing that often what appears as darkness is but a test of your readiness to trust in and to share the Light."

St. Michael's loving words have reverberated in my mind and my heart many times since that glorious night of epiphany. They have remained a constant reminder that what often presents itself to me in the form of challenges, darkness, doubt, and fear are but an opportunity for me to trust in and to share my interior Light.

Only love is real. Everything else is an illusion that is presented to us as a gift, to help us discover this truth.

Only love is real.

"The artist is meant to put the objects of this world together in such a way that through them you will experience that light, that radiance which is the light of our consciousness and which all things both hide and, when properly looked upon, reveal. The hero journey is one of the universal patterns through which that radiance shows brightly. What I think is that a good life is one hero journey after another. Over and over again, you are called to the realm of adventure, you are called to new horizons. Each time, there is the same problem: do I dare? And then if you do dare, the dangers are there, and the help also, and the fulfillment or the fiasco. There's always the possibility of a fiasco. But there's also the possibility of bliss."

-American author,

Joseph Campbell

(1904 – 1987)

Chapter Eight
Epilogue

When I asked the Angels how they would like to close this book, they gave me a not too wordy, yet sincere response:

"Job well done, Dana!"

That's kind of short, don't you think? I asked. "Doesn't seem like much of an ending after all of this time together."

Like a chorus of Angelic tones speaking in one fluid motion, I heard them say, "We'd like to add a little something more."

I smiled inside and said, "That's more like it."

Dana, please ask everyone to replace *your* name, with ***their name*** in our opening statement.   Like this; "Job well done _____!" Just ask them to fill in the blank and then read it out loud."

Obviously a bit chattier than I originally thought, they continued, "You see, Dana, despite what you angels in human form may have been taught to believe while incarnated on earth, this is the way in which **everyone** is greeted upon the return Home."

Each expression of the One, who for a short time is wearing human flesh, chooses to map their return Home according to the scenic tour that each has chosen to take while living on the earth plane. Granted, some portions of the road of human Life are quite bumpy and full of potholes, but overall, there's lots of beauty to be seen even when the road isn't perfectly smooth.   It's up to each driver to see the beauty all around them. It's easy to see the splendor of God along a road paved without challenges.   It's in learning to find the treasure at the bottom of a pothole that the greatest blessings are to be found!"

Until our next volume," they continued, "please remind the reader that the years between their earth birth and their Homecoming are full of twisty turning roads paved with love, loss, healing, heartache, triumph, adventure, and joyful experiences that help to create a human life of learning and spiritual growth.   There are no 'right' roads or 'wrong roads' … because *all* roads lead Home, Dana."

In closing, we would like to say, "May the Journey toward Home be filled with a remembrance that Love is the true nature of all living things. From Love you were born and to love you will all one day return. And…if you should ever tire of navigating life alone, we're happy to go along for the ride."

With love,

The Angels of Light

A Word from My Teammates

To me, one of the most beautiful aspects of earthly life is the perfect placement of friends who join us along any given stretch of the Hero's Journey.

Here, I would like to give voice to four of my favorite fellow life adventurers, as they talk to us of their experience in helping the Angels bring this book to life:

Let us begin with Sister Irene Mary:

My earliest memory of Angels occurred when I was a small child at my mother's knee. She taught me these opening words:

Angel of God my Guardian dear
     To Whom God's love commits me here
     Ever this day be at my side
     To light, to guard, to rule and guide…

My next lesson came at Aquinas College in Grand Rapids, Michigan. Here I had a Dominican Priest explain that Angels are Messengers, and he highly encouraged us to call on our Angels frequently.

When Denise asked me to be one of the editors of this book I quickly said yes, knowing that I would have the opportunity to learn even more about Angels.

Now that I have completed my editorial task, I am happy to say that I have thoroughly enjoyed this journey. Not only did I gain more knowledge about Angels, but I know I have gained "heart" knowledge about these Celestial Beings. This book made me feel "comfortable" with the idea of having these Angelic Helpers to call on. Thank you, Denise, for this opportunity to deepen my faith.

And now a word from David Fix:

"Creating the Mystic Angel cards was a work of discovery for me. I hadn't done much work with angels before, and I hadn't created images like the angels before either. The first two months of trying to create an angel were very frustrating. I had 15 prototypes and I didn't like any of them. My first awakening came when Denise visited me in a dream and used her magic wand to circle my wrist with a ring of sparkles. A few weeks later, in a swirl of complete experimentation, I created an image of the angel named Azrael. I was completely surprised and amazed! Wow. I could hardly believe it. It was like a light switched on. After that, I would ask each angel to reveal itself. Sometimes I thought, "Oh, you want to be this way. Perfect!" Other times I would think, "Are you sure you want to look like that? I kind of thought you should look different. Ok, have it your way." When Denise first used the angels in a group meeting, I was amazed at how strongly the angels interacted with the group. Each time I blindly selected an angel that night, I already knew which one it was going to be. It was one of the few instances in my life where I felt a strong and immediate connection between my intuition and a higher realm. It was powerful. I continue to work with the angels and realize their presence more; I feel like I've met 33 new friends."

…and Eunice Norwood:

I was excited when Dana asked me to proof her book….. I learn so much about myself when I read anything she writes. As expected, I "listened" to the messages she presented and grew inside.

As I proofed the messages from the angels it felt wrong, somehow, to change the words the angels had presented to Dana. As soon as this thought entered my mind, I felt my angels around having a good laugh at me and they told me how much they enjoyed my silliness. From then on, the "job" was lighter and even more enjoyable.

Thank you, Dana, for this joyous pleasure. I love you.

Last but certainly not least, Wendy Mersman:

I have been so blessed to work with Denise for quite a few years. I love her wonderful personality which comes out in everything she touches. Even small things as bringing a smile to your face with her emails or knowing just when to say the right words that will make your day.

Creating for Denise is both easy and hard. Her words are so beautiful that it is easy to visualize and illustrate them. But … her words are so beautiful that often I feel the images are inadequate.

I was so excited when she gave me another opportunity to layout her new book. I knew it would be just as delightful as the last. Struggling with finding just the right images to go with her enchanting words, I, once again, experienced Denise's gifted timing and the divine intervention that I needed.

Thank you, Denise, for all you do.

Insights into a Year of Mystic Angels

"Just holding "A Year of Mystic Angels" in my hands created a quiet opening to Grace and the Angelic Realm in my heart. And in this silence I heard their meaningful words of Self-love, Joyous expression, and Unconditional support for us as we walk this earth journey. Denise has created with Mystic Angels an inspiring and informative lesson plan enabling us to easily open up to the Helpful Beings in our lives."

-Minnie Kansman, author of Spirit Gardens: Rekindling our Nature Connection,

minniekansman.com

"When you walk into the energetic space that is you--reading and processing this wonderful book--you'll feel around you the manifestation of a beautiful, personal temple of love, healing and wisdom. It is populated by the entities in the book as well as your own guides, teachers, angels and loved ones in spirit who are supporting your journey to enlightenment. Give thanks for this sacred space in time and drink in all the nourishment this book has to offer. It is outstanding!"

-Rev. Laura H. MacLachlan

"This amazing book will help you understand that Angels are very real, even if you cannot see them, and they will help you in your daily life if you will just ask. Denise teaches us that Angelic help is only for the special, and that you are special."

-Bob Huttinga, PA

A portion of the proceeds from the sale of Denise's published works goes to her charitable organization, Gathering Thunder Foundation. To learn more, please visit: www.GatheringThunderFoundation.org

Books by Denise:

"Meditations from the Temple Within" - Guided Meditation CD and Journaling Workbook

"Embracing the Mystic Within" - A Personal Journey Toward Spiritual Awakening

"The Journey of Light" - Walking the Reiki Path

"A Year of Mystic Angels" - Guidance from the Celestial High*ways for Intuitive Kids from 2 to 102

Visualization CD's by Denise:

"Meditations from the Temple Within" - Guided Meditation CD and Journaling Workbook

"Beyond the Veil Lies ... a Mystic Journey" - The Meditations

"Journey to The Temple Within" - Meeting Your Guardian Angels

"The Reiki Path" - Meeting Your Reiki Guides

"The Athlete Within" - Accessing your Energy Source

Denise's books and CD's are available at your favorite local bookstore and for digital download at CDbaby.com, Amazon.com and iTunes.com

Join Denise via Internet TV and Radio!

Each Monday evening at 8:00 PM EST, Denise hosts a weekly internet television show entitled, "Mystic Journeys" on channel 4 of the Soul's Journey TV: www.SoulsJourney.tv.

Wednesday evenings at 8 PM EST, finds Denise hosting her weekly internet radio show, "Balancing Heaven and Earth," on Soul's Journey Radio: www.SoulsJourneyRadio.com.

Oracle Cards by Denise:

"The Mystic Angels Empowerment Deck"